How to Convert Your
**Volkswagen T4/T5
Into a Camper Van**

How to Convert Your Volkswagen T4/T5 Into a Camper Van

LAWRENCE BUTCHER

THE CROWOOD PRESS

First published in 2015 by
The Crowood Press Ltd
Ramsbury, Marlborough
Wiltshire SN8 2HR

www.crowood.com

This impression 2019

© Lawrence Butcher 2015

All rights reserved. No part of this publication may be reproduced or transmitted in any form or by any means, electronic or mechanical, including photocopy, recording, or any information storage and retrieval system, without permission in writing from the publishers.

British Library Cataloguing-in-Publication Data
A catalogue record for this book is available from the British Library.

ISBN 978 1 84797 879 0

Disclaimer
Safety is of the utmost importance in every aspect of an automotive workshop. The practical procedures and the tools and equipment used in automotive workshops are potentially dangerous. Tools should be used in strict accordance with the manufacturer's recommended procedures and current health and safety regulations. The author and publisher cannot accept responsibility for any accident or injury caused by following the advice given in this book.

Typeset by Servis Filmsetting Ltd, Stockport, Cheshire
Printed and bound in India by Parksons graphics Pvt. Ltd.

contents

acknowledgements	6
1 introduction and buying guide	7
2 planning and other considerations	18
3 chopping holes	25
4 ground work	42
5 making a box a home	52
6 beds and seating	71
7 gas and water	88
8 electricity	97
9 useful extras	116
index	127

acknowledgements

Special thanks are due to Sam and Laura Jeffery of VWorks, a VW restoration and conversion specialist based in Kent. Sam learnt his trade working for a large camper van conversion company before setting up his own business. The company works on every type of classic VW, completing everything from interior makeovers to ground up restorations. They have even converted a Split-Screen camper into a mobile tea shop, complete with opening roof and side counter. The project detailed in these pages would not have been possible without Sam's guidance and assistance, not to mention use of workshop space. It is thanks to his knowledge and input that the conversion undertaken here should be within the abilities of most competent home enthusiasts. More information and details of the projects undertaken can be found at vworks.co.uk.

Thanks must also be given to Mike Devine of Cheshire Motor Caravans, who provided some of the major components in the van, including the roof and bed. The company was always helpful and provided answers whenever a question arose as to the best way to fit a particular component. If you are looking to convert a T5 or T4, CMC are a good bet for parts. Nearly all of their kit is designed and built in-house and is excellent quality. Check out their website at c-m-c.org.

VW's range of vans have always been popular as campers. VOLKSWAGEN

1
introduction and buying guide

The saying 'home is where you park it' was coined around the image of hippies and beatniks wandering the countryside in VW vans through the heady days of the Summer of Love. Times may have changed, but the appeal of a mobile home away from home still appeals to many. In order to fulfil this yearning, some opt for a behemoth motorhome, while others lean towards the scourge of the holiday traffic jam, a caravan. But by far the most sensible solution is a van-based camper, providing sufficient interior space to prevent claustrophobia, but not so large that you need planning permission to park it.

There is a plethora of different-sized, pre-converted camper vans from a variety of manufacturers available; the most predominantly available are those based on VW's range of commercial vehicles. If you decide to purchase a ready-to-go camper, hopefully this book will still be of use in determining the differences between the host of specifications available, and, if buying a used conversion, what problems you should look out for. However, this type of camper van comes with a hefty price tag. At the very top of the tree, a new VW-produced California camper will set you back north of £50,000, while conversions from the likes of Danbury are between £30,000 and £40,000. Second-hand values are also strong, with the starting point for good-quality T4-based vehicles at around the £10,000 mark and T5s at £15–20,000. Compared with the prices of the vehicles upon which they are based, this is a big premium; for example, in the 2013 market a low-mileage 2007 VW T5 panel van can be had for around £7,000.

This gulf in values makes the option of converting a van

T5 California. VOLKSWAGEN

introduction and buying guide

yourself an attractive one. If you have a modicum of DIY skills, you can save a considerable amount of cash in your pursuit of camper-van Nirvana. In addition, you will have complete control over the form and features of the end product. To help you achieve this, the aim of this book is to cover all of the key aspects of converting a VW T4 or T5 panel van into a camper. It will help you ascertain the basics of buying a modern van, what to look out for and which models are most appropriate as a basis for conversion. All of the jobs undertaken to complete the conversion will be within the abilities of a competent DIY mechanic with access to basic hand and power tools.

WHY A MODERN VW?

After nearly 40 years of following a cab forward–rear engine design for its vans, in 1990 VW finally developed a front-engined platform light commercial vehicle, dubbed the T4. While many say that the vans of the modern generation lack the character of VW's older offerings, notably the Split and Bay Windows of the 1950s and 1960s, there is no disputing their practicality. In recent years this new generation of vans has developed a strong following amongst VW enthusiasts looking for the renowned VW build quality and style, without the hassle of running a classic car.

Driven back to back, the difference between a T25 and a T4 is like night and day; where the T25 feels very much like a 'van', the experience of the T4 is much more akin to driving a large family car. Move up to a T5 and the difference is even more startling, with levels of refinement and comfort that will surprise drivers used to commercials from other manufacturers. It would be fair to say that vans from other manufacturers such as the Ford Transit and the Vauxhall Vivaro fulfil essentially the same role as a VW Transporter, but they do not carry the same cachet in terms of brand identity.

BUYING A VAN

The Basics

Some T4s have been around for over twenty years now, and the earliest T5s are over a decade old, so there are many well-worn examples on the second-hand market. While this means that there are some good bargains to be had, it also follows that there are some that are best avoided. The biggest factor to consider when buying either model is that the majority of vans will have been used by tradesmen, or, in the case of Caravelles, by taxi or executive transport companies. This invariably means that they will have led a hard life. In some cases, this is not necessarily a bad thing – a diesel that has been well cared for can happily see the far side of 200,000 miles, provided the correct service intervals have been adhered to.

A quick search of the online classifieds will yield many hundreds of vans, to suit all budgets. A rough and ready T4 can be had for a few hundred pounds, while a nearly new top-spec T5.5 will cost upwards of £20,000. It is important to bear in mind your overall budget for the conversion when buying your base vehicle, but buy the best you can afford. While it is not a major issue to have to save a little longer for an interior trinket, it is a much bigger problem if your base vehicle turns out to be a money pit, requiring constant remedial maintenance.

Service History

It goes without saying that a comprehensive service history is a must with any second-hand vehicle. If you are buying a newer van, a dealer-based history is especially desirable, but for older vans there is nothing wrong with work having been undertaken by independent garages. Look for the service interval stamps in the service book, but also take time to study any receipts and invoices. These will give you the nitty gritty of the work that has been undertaken. The key jobs to look out for are the timing belt and oil change services. On a higher-mileage vehicle, a new clutch is a desirable feature as these are expensive to change and wear out after heavy use. Two vans may look identical and be offered at a similar price, but if one has had these major services undertaken it is a much better value purchase. As a reference, cambelts should be changed every 60,000 miles or four years.

BUYING A T4

Discounting various oddities produced for specialist industries, the T4 was produced in five main body types based on the variants first introduced with the Split-Screen in the 1950s. The biggest sellers were the panel vans, which are pure commercials without any windows other than those around the cab. Variants referred to as Kombis are also commonplace; these feature windows in the front half of the load bay area and a second row of seats. The final variant of interest to the potential converter are those that were intended for use as minibuses, fitted with all-around glazing (which makes life easier from a conversion perspective). These are known as Caravelles or Multivans and often feature a much higher level of interior trim than panel vans or Kombis.

Purely as a point of interest, VW also produced both single- and dual-cab pick-up variants. There were two standard wheelbases for all transporters: a short version of 115in (2,920mm) and a long variant at 131in (3,320mm).

There was one major facelift to the T4, in 1996, when a re-shaped, longer front end was introduced in order to accommodate a six-cylinder VR6 engine. Initially, only Caravelles and Multivans were available with the longer nose, since these were the only models fitted with the VR6 engine. The commercial variants continued to be produced with the shorter nose until 1999. However, campers and other specialist vehicles produced between 1994 and 1999 may have either the short or the long nose, depending on which model was used as the base vehicle. In keeping with the Type 2's naming convention, the short- and long-nose versions are also informally known as T4a and T4b, respectively.

Engines

The very earliest versions of the T4 were available with an 1800cc petrol engine, however, from both a power and economy perspective, these are best avoided. In truth, this

introduction and buying guide

T4 California. VOLKSWAGEN

applies to the majority of the petrol-engined vans. The diesels, while they are less refined, provide better economy and greater low-end torque. For the T4, the diesel options ranged from a non-turbocharged 1.9-litre through to the range topping 2.5-litre. The non-turbo 1.9-litre is best avoided as its paltry 61 PS output makes for painful progress when fully laden. The best choices are either the 68PS 1.9 TD or the range-topping 2.5-litre, five-cylinder TDi, which churns out an impressive 151PS. In terms of economy, a carefully driven 1.9 TD can return in the region of 40mpg, while the larger 2.5 TDi will give 30–35mpg average consumption.

Gearbox

Four-cylinder variants of the T4 used a five-speed manual gearbox based on the unit found in a number of VW's road cars, including the Corrado and the Golf. For the five- and six-cylinder motors, a stronger unit was developed to handle the extra torque. The TDi variants were also fitted with a dual mass flywheel, made up of two key parts – one bolted to the engine, the other to the clutch – linked by springs and friction pads, to help damp engine vibrations. These can prove problematic in higher-mileage vehicles as the mating between the two flywheel halves breaks down. One tell-tale sign of this happening is a juddering in first and reverse gears; replacement is expensive, at around £800. An automatic transmission was also available but is an uncommon option; there is a good reason for this, as it had a considerable impact on fuel economy. The automatic transmission also suffered from reliability issues, with many failing after fewer than 100,000 miles due to problems with the torque converter. It is also worth mentioning that the T4 was available in Syncro form, featuring VW's four-wheel-drive system. A Syncro is a rare beast indeed, but will provide unrivalled traction, so, if you have visions of winter touring in the Alps, it could be worth seeking one out.

Chassis

Given their age, most T4s will have seen some pretty substantial miles; fortunately, they are pretty sturdy. After a life of heavy lifting, the suspension will more than likely have taken a pounding and broken rear springs are a common occurrence, often thanks to the builder's overly optimistic opinions of their load-carrying capacity. One indication of a cracked spring is the van sitting unevenly at the rear. The

introduction and buying guide

front suspension is of the torsion bar variety, meaning that it is really easy to lower. However, this can place a lot of strain on the lower ball joints, and this may become apparent in the form of a loud knock, which may occur as the wheel hits a bump or pothole. As with any second-hand vehicle, it is important to take a good look at all the damper and other suspension components and to check them for wear. Front and rear discs are easy to inspect, but it should be noted that, prior to 1996, some models only featured drums at the rear.

Bodywork

With the introduction of the facelifted T4, in 1996, VW also greatly improved the rust-proofing on its vans. Pre-1996 models can suffer from considerable quantities of rot, particularly if they have not been well looked after. The most susceptible areas are around the rear wheel arches and the back of the inner front arch, as these are great dirt traps. It is also important to look out for any signs of body-damage repairs – ill-fitting doors and mismatched paint are the dead giveaways. Particular areas to check are the front chassis rails under the bonnet and the area behind the rear bumper – any creases here are an indication that the van has taken a whack. With the number of T4s on the market, buying a beaten-up one on the cheap is a false economy; any money you save initially will soon be eaten up in repair bills.

BUYING A T5

With the introduction of the T5, in 2003, VW raised the bar for commercial vehicle comfort and road manners up another notch. Although it was more evolutionary than revolutionary in its appearance, under the skin the new van was a different beast all together. It introduced previously unheard of levels of driving comfort, with the result that a T5 feels just like a tall estate car from the driver's seat. One of the most significant improvements related to the engine mounting; this engine was carried on a separate sub-frame and this greatly reduced cabin noise.

The T5 underwent a major facelift in 2009. This saw the vehicle cosmetics brought right up to date, the most noticeable difference being a restyled front end. There is no denying that the appearance of the later model vans is far more striking, however, this comes at a considerable price premium over older models.

Interior of a T5 California. VOLKSWAGEN

introduction and buying guide

T5 California sleeping area. VOLKSWAGEN

Engines

Volkswagen stuck with the existing direct-injection diesel engine configuration – commonly referred to as the PD family of engines – found in the last-of-the-line T4s. From 2003 to 2010 two variants of the four-cylinder diesel were available in 85PS or 104PS form, while the 2.5-litre TDI was available with either a 130PS output or a whopping 174PS. In 2010, VW revamped the range and began offering its new-four cylinder 2.0-litre TDi engines, which also marked the demise of the 2.5. The new oil burner was available in five variants: four single turbo units offering outputs ranging from 84PS to 140PS and a twin-turbo pushing out 179PS.

Four petrol engines were also offered, although these are rare – for various reasons. The smaller-capacity units provided very little benefit over their diesel counterparts while the larger motors drank fuel like it was going out of fashion. The 2003–10 models were available with a 2-litre naturally aspirated petrol and a stonking great 3.2 V6 pushing out 235PS. Meanwhile, from 2010 two 2.0-litre four cylinders appeared, one a direct-injection naturally aspirated 116PS unit and a turbo-charged variant producing 204PS.

Gearbox

Although the T5's transmission is generally reliable, there are two key areas where problems are known to develop. The first, as with the T4, is the failure of the dual mass flywheel, which can result in juddering. A good test for this is to reverse the van slowly uphill, which will highlight the issue. The second is worn drive-shaft splines, particularly on the right-hand side due to a lack of lubrication. It is hard to check for this, but it is worth asking the seller if they have experienced any issues and, if so, whether any remedial work has been undertaken.

Post-2009 T5s are also available with VW's dual-clutch DSG transmission, which combines the ease of use of an

introduction and buying guide

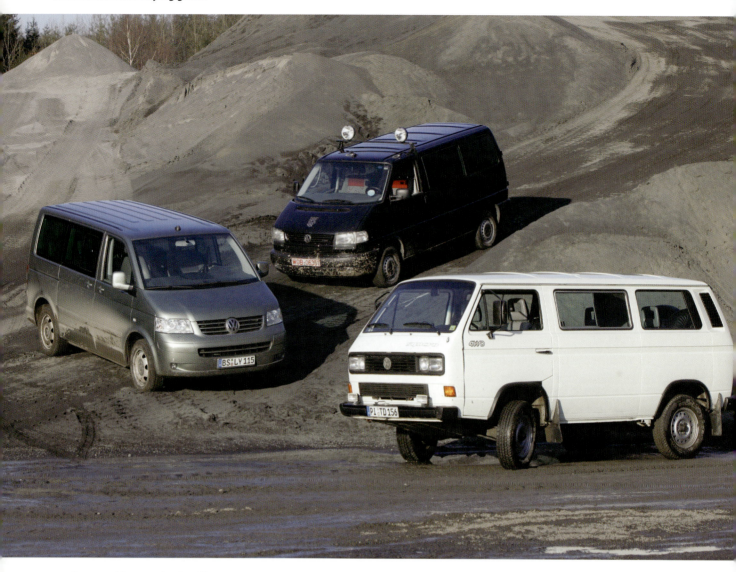

Syncro models are rare but desirable. VOLKSWAGEN

automatic transmission with the response of a manual. At its heart is a two-piece main shaft, with one shaft section running inside the other. Each shaft carries three gears with odd-numbered gears on one and even numbers on the other. Attached to each shaft is a multi-plate wet clutch, one running inside the other, with the engagement of each clutch being controlled by a hydraulic circuit. Gear selection is also controlled by hydraulic servo motors and the vehicle's control electronics govern overall operation. The theory is that the ECU determines which gear is likely to be needed next and then pre-engages it. As soon as the driver initiates a shift, the clutches engage and disengage, selecting the next gear with minimal lag. In operation, the system is excellent, providing nearly imperceptible shifts.

Reliability is normally good with the DSG boxes, with faults that developed on early iterations having been resolved through manufacturer recalls. However, when considering a higher-mileage vehicle, it is important to weigh up the benefits of the sublime shifting against potential costly repair bills if things do go wrong.

Chassis

With the T5, VW departed from the torsion bar front/coil spring rear suspension system of the T4 in favour of a MacPherson strut set-up at the front. The most common problem with T5s that have been used as trade vehicles is broken rear springs. These are easily replaced but it is worth checking their condition by looking at the van from the rear to see if it is sitting square, or simply inspecting the springs in situ. The rest of the checks relating to the chassis are similar to those that you would undertake on any other vehicle. When driving, listen out for clunks and rattles; a rattle when going over a bump is most likely to reflect wear in the anti-roll bar mounts – a cheap fix but a good bargaining point. The suspension ball joints can also wear, and this will cause a loud noise when you hit a hole. One oddity of the T5 is that some owners have experienced squeaking or clonking steering columns, with no real solution available bar replacing the entire column (which is of course costly).

Another area to check is the shocks. Over time these can leak, so look for any signs of fluid on the shock bodies.

introduction and buying guide

Bodywork

T5s were very well rust-proofed from the factory so body corrosion is not common. If there are any signs of rust, it is most likely due to poorly repaired accident damage. On vehicles with colour-coded bumpers, it is a good idea to check that they are either factory-fitted or have been painted properly. Painting plastic bumpers is notoriously difficult and the correct procedures need to be followed in order to obtain a long-lasting finish. If the paint is starting to flake, it will only get worse so the expense of repainting (at least £500) should be factored into your negotiations. One problem suffered by some earlier T5s was water ingress through the window seals, which can lead to rust in areas such as the door steps and can also cause electrical problems. If it is raining when you take a test drive it is easy to check for leaks; otherwise, examine the cab floor area carefully for signs of damp.

One problem to look out for on panel vans is dents on the exterior caused by careless loading and unloading of various objects. In the case of the van featured in this book, there was damage to the rear window area (which was not glazed) due to long items not fitting in the van. Fortunately, this was not an issue as the area in question was earmarked for removal and a window was to be fitted. It is also common for the bottom edge of the tailgate to be damaged if items have been left sticking out as it is shut.

Interior

T5s came with a variety of interior configurations, all of which are pretty hard-wearing. The most common set-up, particularly in Transporter variants, featured a driver's seat and twin passenger seats, generally trimmed in cloth fabric. The twin passenger seats feature a very useful storage space underneath that is ideal for hiding valuables.

Far less common are Transporters with a single passenger seat. On higher-spec vans, such as Sportlines and Caravelles, leather-trimmed seats were an option, along with other niceties such as arm-rests. Obviously, rear seating was also provided in some models, but, if you are undertaking a camper conversion, this will most likely be surplus to requirements.

The only real issues to look out for when it comes to checking the interior relate to general wear and tear. Torn seat bolsters, for example, can be expensive to repair, although there are plenty of second-hand seats available on the market. One foolish decision by VW was to specify a light-coloured front headlining, which marked incredibly easily and was hard to clean. It was not the best call for a working vehicle.

Moving into the rear of the van, it is very common for the hardboard side panels to be damaged due to careless loading. This can be a problem if you plan to retain the panels, although carpet lining can hide a plethora of sins.

Optional Extras

Standard T5 Transporters often came with a pretty basic specification, although the list of optional extras was quite extensive. Among the more desirable extras are cruise control, electric windows and air-conditioning, which can add a fair bit to a van's value. It is worth checking that they are working properly. The air-con, for example, should blow nice and cold. If it does not, it probably only needs a re-gas, but it can be difficult to identify whether the problem might be due to other issues. It is possible to retro-fit cruise control to some vans, depending on the electronics control unit that was fitted in the factory. As a rule of thumb, if a van has electric windows and electric mirrors, it is probably capable of accepting cruise control.

On later vans, the number of available extras increased, with the more popular additions being satellite navigation and reversing sensors, both worthwhile options if you can find them. However, it is not worth paying a large premium for such features and both can be quite easily retro-fitted without excessive expense.

The 1.9 TDi engine is the staple of the T4 and 5 range.

Brake fluid reservoir.

The chassis plate on the right-hand side of the engine bay gives vehicle details.

introduction and buying guide

Check the coolant level – mayonnaise deposits indicate head gasket issues.

Check the power steering fluid level, if fitted.

Get underneath the van and check the condition of the suspension and chassis.

OUR VAN

The subject of this book, sourced through the Auto Trader website, was no beauty queen when it was purchased. When your budget is tight you have to hunt out the best deals. While our van did not exactly fit the 'desired spec' list, it was a good buy.

It is a 2004 T28, featuring the lowly 84PS, 1.9 TDi engine. The mileage was a little on the high side, at just over 150,000, but this was made up for by an exceptional service history. The two most important factors were that it had a tailgate and had not been used as a builder's van. Having looked at a number of vehicles, some of which were several thousand pounds more, this one had the best condition bodywork and had evidently led an easy life. It had also benefited from a new clutch and timing belt 12 months previously. Costing just over £5,000, it provided a good starting point for a budget-conscious conversion into a fully functioning camper van.

It was not all positive. There were a few niggling problems to take care of; for example, the front anti-roll bar bushes needed replacement as did the lower suspension bushes. We also decided that an exterior makeover was in order, to help make the finished article look as far removed from a 'white van' as possible. This involved several days of rubbing down and masking up to prepare the body for paint. A two-tone scheme was picked, to mimic the campers of old – the blue colour is one that was used on VW's T25 commercials. This was extra work that was not strictly necessary, but the end result was well worth the effort.

introduction and buying guide

Our van!

Note any dents – ours were in the tailgate.

introduction and buying guide

Most interiors will look like this.

Ply lining has protected the sides.

The van undergoing a colour change.

The end result after a lot of hard work and effort.

2 planning and other considerations

Sitting down and planning your conversion is a really fun part of the project.

Planning your camper is one of the most enjoyable parts of the conversion, beyond actually using the finished product. Additionally, having a clear idea of what you want out of the conversion will make life a lot easier when it comes to budgeting. While this will invariably be a best guess, at least you will have some idea of the financial commitment needed.

What do you want to use the van for? Are you looking for a day van, which will accommodate the odd night's camping, or do you want a full-on expedition-spec tourer, with every amenity under the sun? To a large degree, this, along with budget, will dictate the direction that your conversion takes. For example, if you want your van to double as a people carrier and a day/weekend camper, it may be worthwhile opting for a Caravelle that has additional seating and incorporates a pop-top roof. This would provide a balance between practicality and camping accommodation. Conversely, if the van is to be used solely as a camper, you can go all out on the interior fittings and fixtures to make it as comfortable a place as possible.

For some people, the ability to continue to use the van for its original purpose – transporting large objects – may still be important. In which case, the addition of kitchen units may not be the best approach as these will impinge considerably on load space. However, adding a pop-top will not and will instantly double the space available. There is nothing wrong with a very basic conversion, consisting of just a rock and roll bed and some storage boxes, if it fulfils your needs. I used this van in just such a state for a two-week trip around Europe, with a simple rock and roll bed providing ample comfort for two.

The beauty of undertaking a conversion yourself is that you can choose the exact layout and level of functionality that will suit your needs, and not be tied into someone else's interpretation. For example, if you are into a particular type of activity, such as rock climbing or watersports, you can tailor the interior to incorporate dedicated storage space for your equipment. There is also the option of making a modular interior, where the units can be easily removed to create more space when needed. All sorts of things can be done with the interior of a humble van if you let your imagination run wild.

A modular fibreglass kitchen unit.

planning and other considerations

A roller or tambour door is a useful option where space is at a premium.

The use of contrasting wood and man-made finishes can be effective.

A very traditional layout.

Simple but striking.

BUDGETING

Money is no one's favourite subject, but the reality is that it will invariably dictate the type and pace of your conversion. While it is not impossible, it is very hard to account for every single cost that is likely to be encountered during a build, but it is possible to get a good idea of how much each area of the van will set you back. Start out with a clear, and more importantly realistic, budget in mind. The way you plan to approach the conversion will also affect the way in which the budget is used. If you have plenty of time, it is possible to buy all of the parts piecemeal, with large expenditures, such as a

Pop-top roofs make great sense.

19

planning and other considerations

A factory-made T4 conversion.

The sky is the limit if customizing is your thing.

More akin to a high-end kitchen than a camper van.

- Carpet lining and flooring: DIY fit c.£300, professional c.£600.
- Pop-top roof: good quality, DIY fit £2,000–2,500, professional c.£3,000.
- Appliances: 12V fridge, cooker, sink, running water, £500–1,000, depending on specifications.
- Electrical components: 12V–240V power-management system, leisure battery, wiring and so on, £400–600.
- Interior units: furniture ply, hinges and fixings, £500.
- Bed: £300–1,000 depending on specification of bed.
- Seating and upholstery: swivel seat bases and upholstery for rear seats, DIY £500; add £250 for professional upholstery.

This gives an idea of the costs for the basic conversion items. If you start to get into lots of trick extras, such as entertainment systems and gas or diesel heating, the costs will increase considerably. However, components such as these can be easily added at a later date once the essentials are in place. It is perfectly feasible to build a fully functioning camper, using a base vehicle with reasonable mileage, for between £10,000 and £12,000; it is no small amount of money but still considerably less than it would cost to buy a ready-converted van, and far less than a similar-aged VW California, for example.

TOOLS

It is easy to overlook, but having the right tools for a job makes life an awful lot simpler and, ultimately, leads to a better-quality job. The old saying that a poor workman blames his tools is right to a degree, but 'the right tool for the job' also rings true. A fully trained cabinet-maker may be able to produce a beautiful bespoke interior with just traditional hand tools, but they will have spent a life time learning how to use them. While you will not be able to replicate the results of their skill with even the best power tools, you will save a lot of frustration and time; for example, cutting out a window aperture is a lot less frustrating using a jigsaw rather than a hacksaw. Good tools cost money, but in the long run they are a worthwhile investment and once your conversion is complete, you can always sell them again to recoup some costs. If you shell out £500 on some specific tools, it will be money well spent.

While someone considering taking on a conversion is likely to have a fairly decent array of tools already, this advice assumes you have none and looks at some of the bare necessities.

Mechanic's Tools

A decent set of basic mechanic's tools is a must for anyone planning to work on a vehicle. Although hopefully you will not have to get too involved with the oily bits of your van, some of the jobs, such as fitting the bed and removing the seats, will make this necessary. At the very least you need a good set of metric sockets, quarter- and half-inch drive, a set of combination spanners, and items such as pliers and a good ball-peen hammer. Splashing out on top-of-the-range

pop-top roof or the kitchen appliances, being spread out to lessen the financial sting. It is also imperative to have some form of contingency budget. If you hit a snag, or find out later that you really need a particular component and do not have the cash to buy it, it can stop your build in its tracks.

What are the likely costs involved in converting a van? Based on current prices, they can be roughly broken down as follows:

- Van: T5 transporter, £4,000–15,000 depending on age and mileage. Models such as Caravelles, 4-Motions and so on, command a considerable premium.
- Windows: all-around glass, DIY fit c.£600.

planning and other considerations

kit is not necessary, but you should try to get the best quality you can afford. The tools offered by ranges such as Halford's and Draper Professional provide a good compromise between cost and quality.

There are also a few specialist tools that will come in handy. For example, the load-bay tie-down eyelets and seatbelt mounts are attached using splined head bolts; these are not the standard Torx type and have a 12-spline design. Also, if you are planning on doing your servicing at home, a decent oil-filter wrench and oil-catch can are worthwhile investments.

You will also be working under the vehicle, and it is not recommended to rely on the standard scissor jack for support; a two-ton vehicle landing on your head will not be good for your health. A decent trolley jack and axle stands will set you back approximately £100, but are worth it for peace of mind.

The jigsaw will become your best friend.

Power Tools

There are a number of stages during the conversion of a van where the right power tools will help you. The bare requirements are a cordless drill/driver and a jigsaw. You will need to do a lot of drilling and screwing, particularly when building your interior units, so it is advisable to purchase a good-quality 12V or 18V cordless drill. Companies such as Screwfix often have very good offers on these and stock high-quality brands such as Makita and DeWalt, with an entry-level drill costing around £100. When you purchase a drill make sure you get a good selection of driver bits, particularly Phillips and Pozi-drive types. Although they look similar, cross-head screws come in these two main varieties and, if you use the wrong driver bit, the bit will slip when you are trying to drive the screw. Most screw packs will say which bit to use; for example, screws marked PZ2 will use a Pozi-drive size 2.

A useful accessory to complement your newly acquired drill is a good-quality set of hole saws. These will come in very handy over the course of the conversion, particularly when it comes to creating holes for power sockets and in the metalwork of the van. It is definitely not worth skimping on quality when it comes to hole saws, as this will only lead to frustration. Buy the best bi-metal saws you can afford, so that you will be able to cut through both wood and metal. Offerings from manufacturers such as Bosch and DeWalt are a good bet. Good-quality saws will cut easily and, more importantly, cleanly, resulting in a much better level of final fit and finish.

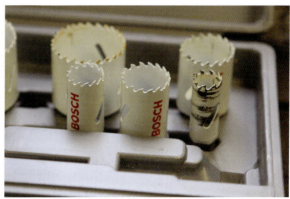

Hole saws make light work of metal and wood.

Another 'must-have' power tool is a good-quality circular saw. When it comes to cutting long straight edges, such as those that will be necessary when constructing interior units or making bed boards, a circular saw is the only way to go. It may be possible to do it by hand, or with a jigsaw, but it will be much harder to obtain a good finish. A saw of a reasonable quality can be had for £50–100; a tool in this price range would not survive sustained professional use, but it will be more than adequate for occasional DIY use. A good bet is the range of saws produced by the Evolution brand, which start at about £60 and have the benefit of being available with metal-cutting as well as wood-cutting blades. Cordless circular saws are available, but, without spending several hundred pounds, they cannot match the cutting ability of a mains version.

On the subject of blades, most saws will be supplied with a general-purpose, fairly coarse-toothed blade. If you are working with high-quality veneered furniture ply, you should purchase a new blade specifically for this purpose. This will have much finer teeth than a general-purpose blade – around eighty on a 250mm saw – and using one will help prevent chipping the veneer as the blade rips through the wood. Use this blade only for fine work, in order to keep

A router is a necessity for fitting knock-on furniture edging.

planning and other considerations

it as sharp as possible. In terms of longevity, although they cost more than regular blades, tungsten carbide-tipped blades (TCT) will keep their edge much longer.

The final piece of the power tool puzzle is a router. Such a tool is only a necessity if you are going to use knock-on edging for your furniture (*see* Chapter 5), but it can also come in handy for other tasks. A router acts rather like a milling machine, using a rotating bit to remove wood in shapes that would be hard to achieve using hand tools. The bits are interchangeable, with different bits being used to create different profiles. For example, a square-edged groove may be achieved using a slotting bit – a flat-faced cutter that cuts horizontally into the workpiece. These are available in a variety of sizes, but for creating the slot needed to accommodate knock-on edging strips a 3mm cutter is needed.

Routers are available in two main types, plunge or fixed-base. Plunge routers have a spring-loaded base that allows the bit to be pushed down into the wood. The spring-loaded base can also be locked at a specific depth by the user. Plunge routers allow the user to change the bit depth while running, by unlocking the depth release and moving the base in and out. This can be a useful feature where a cut starts in the middle of a piece of wood instead of at the edge. Plunge routers offer more versatility too but are generally more expensive than fixed-base routers and using them with the plunge function enabled can take some mastering.

With a fixed-base router, the user must set the depth of the blade prior to use and it is not adjustable when the router is running. Adjustments are often made by twisting the housing to screw or unscrew the router in the base, thereby moving the router bit up and down. Fixed-base routers are ideal for edge cuts and moulding designs that require straight-line precision. Generally, they are lighter in weight and easier to use than plunge routers. The fixed-base router is a popular choice for beginners and if the only task you need to complete is slotting for edge banding, a fixed machine will be just fine.

TIME

Of course, it is vital to have a good idea of the financial resources that you have available for your camper conversion. However, it must also be remembered that time is a valuable resource; all too often, the money may be available for a project, but the aspiring converter may not have enough time to complete it. It is quite feasible for a professional outfit, with all the right tools available, to turn around a job such as fitting a pop-top roof in a couple of days. The DIY converter should bank on it taking considerably longer. For our conversion, even with a good level of practical experience, working in a spacious workshop and with guidance from an experienced professional (Sam of VWorks), the roof fitting still took the best part of four days to complete.

Overall, our entire conversion – working jobs in and around earning a living – took the best part of a year from start to finish. If you had no other commitments, and all of the parts were available, it would probably be possible for a competent enthusiast to complete all the work within a month to six weeks. However, very few DIY converters have that luxury.

The best order of jobs also needs to be taken into account. Ideally, the conversion should happen in the following order, although obviously this can be adjusted to suit your particular needs and resources:

1. Undertake all extensive bodywork modifications; this includes any paintwork, window fitting and roof fitting.
2. Carpet lining.
3. Flooring.
4. Fitting of bed and swivel seats.
5. Electrical installation.
6. Interior units.
7. Upholstery and trim.

Obviously it makes sense to get all of the cutting and painting out of the way before starting on the furnishing side of the project. Other timetabling, such as fitting the bed prior to the interior units, is less obvious. In this case, it is owing to the width of the bed dictating the width of the interior units, as well as taking into account the practical location of doors and cupboards. Always considering the impact one job will have on another will save time and frustration in the long run.

One final point on the subject of time, which may seem obvious to many: consider the time of year when you start your conversion. Most people do not have a garage large enough to accommodate a van and their work will more than likely have to take place on a driveway. If you are cutting holes in the bodywork, you do not want to be doing it in the rain. It therefore makes sense to start work in the summer months, hopefully ensuring that your van will be weather tight by the time the wetter weather comes around.

MATERIALS

The materials required for each stage of a conversion will be addressed in greater detail in the relevant chapters, but it is worth covering them briefly here. The key requirement of any materials used in a camper is that they should be hard-wearing, as the interior tends to live a tough life.

When it comes to wood, whether for the cupboards or furniture, always buy the best quality you can afford. Decent plywood, which has a degree of water resistance and a good surface finish, is not cheap, but it is worth the expenditure. First, it will remain much more 'stable' than cheap board, meaning that it will not warp as easily over time. Second, good-quality wood will have a decent surface finish, meaning that it will require less sanding and filling to get looking smart.

The same attention should be applied to fixtures such as hinges and drawer runners. Taking drawer runners as an example, they can be bought for a couple of pounds, but will invariably be sticky to operate and rattle. For a few extra pounds, runners with proper bearings will last the test of time and run smoothly and quietly, more than justifying the small increase in expense.

The quality of fabric you choose to use for trimming will also have an impact on the longevity of your van's interior.

planning and other considerations

Again, try to buy the best you can afford. Proper vehicle upholstery material is normally quite thick and has a scrim (thin foam) backing, making it more resistant to abrasion. The same goes for seat foam. Proper upholstery foam is available in a variety of densities and should not collapse and sag over time.

RULES AND REGULATIONS

There are a number of laws and rules that govern the regulation of camper vans. Fortunately, when it comes to building a camper van for private use, there is considerable leeway.

Insurance

It is a simple fact that the majority of big insurance companies are simply not geared up to deal with people who want to alter their vehicles, be they cars or camper vans. It therefore pays to go to a specialist who will be able to cater more precisely to your needs. While there are a number of companies out there, I have always found Herts Insurance Consultants (HIC) to be helpful, understanding and good value. Having insured everything from a street-legal drag-racing Beetle through to classic and modern VW vans with them, I have never found them wanting.

It is important to use a company that understands its clients properly. For example, if you tell a big-name insurer that your van is being converted, they will often only insure it as a regular commercial vehicle (which entails a much higher premium). However, a specialist will ask you what exactly you plan to do to the vehicle, take this into consideration and ensure you have the cover you need. For example, our featured van was insured as a camper from the outset. As the various jobs were completed, the insurance company was informed and the value of the vehicle reassessed. If the worst happens and your van is written off for any reason, if it is only insured as a van, not as a camper, an insurance company is well within its rights to pay out only for a van. Clearly, the valuation will be much less than a camper is worth. By using a specialist that has a knowledge of the market, you should be able to avoid such problems.

Vehicle Reclassification

It is possible to get a van reclassified as a camper van as long as it meets a number of criteria set out by the DVLA. Whether you do this is down to personal choice, but there are some circumstances in which it would be beneficial. The most notable of these relates to government-instigated LEZs (low emissions zones), which prohibit the entry of commercial vehicles that do not meet certain emissions standards unless a punitive fee is paid. All T5s comply with these requirements, but the majority of diesel engine T4s fall foul. Therefore, if your T4 van is still registered as a commercial, you will be liable to pay the charges on entering an LEZ zone.

Some insurance companies will require a vehicle to be re-registered in order to be insured as a camper, with the majority using the DVLA's requirements as a guide.

If you decide that you want to re-register your van as a camper van you need to contact the DVLA. Before doing this, you will need to make sure that your vehicle meets all of the required criteria, which are quite specific:

- Sleeping accommodation: there must be a bed with a minimum length of 6ft or 180cm. The bed must be an integral part of the vehicle living accommodation area. The bed must be permanent or converted from seats (it may fold away during the day). The bed fixtures must be secured directly to the vehicle floor and/or side walls, unless it is over the driver's cab compartment.
- Doors: there must be a horizontal sliding door or an outward-opening rear or side door.
- Seats and tables: there must be a seating area for diners to sit around. The table can be fixed or detachable. The table must mount directly to the vehicle floor or side walls. The table mounting must be secured as a permanent feature, either bolted, screwed or welded. The table itself can be detachable. Seats must be secured directly to the vehicle floor and/or side walls. The seats must be secured as a permanent fixture, either bolted, riveted, screwed or welded. Permanently secured seating must be available for use at a table.
- Water containers: the DVLA does not state any requirements regarding water storage. However, some insurance companies state that the water tank should be mounted onboard, or under the chassis.
- Storage: the vehicle must have at least one cupboard, locker or wardrobe. The cupboard must be an integral part of the living accommodation area. It must be a permanent feature, either bolted, riveted, screwed or welded to the vehicle.
- Cooking: the vehicle must have cooking facilities powered by a fixed gas supply, electric hob or microwave oven. The cooking facilities must be secured directly to the vehicle floor or side wall and be a permanent feature. Gas and electric hobs must have a minimum of two cooking rings. Microwave ovens must have a power source. Gas cooking facilities with remote fuel supplies must have the gas supply pipe permanently secured to the vehicle structure while gas cooking facilities with remote fuel supplies should have the gas bottle, fuel reservoir secured to the vehicle structure.
- Exterior: the vehicle must have at least one side window.

When your conversion is complete, contact the DVLA and inform it in order to change the classification on the log book to 'Motor Caravan'. When you send the log book to the DVLA to carry out the change (DVLA, Swansea, SA99 1BA), include a covering letter outlining the work that you have done and at least ten pictures showing the work. If everything is in order you should face no problems. However, if the DVLA is not satisfied, they may ask for the vehicle to be checked by a DVLA inspector to confirm the details.

Once the vehicle has been converted and reclassified, it is important to notify your insurance company that this has happened. Even if they were happy to class your van as a camper for insurance purposes, if the information on your insurance document does not match up with that on the log book, you could face problems in the event of a claim.

planning and other considerations

SAFETY

Working on vehicles can be dangerous, so it is important to be aware of the risks and to take steps to mitigate them.

Working Under the Van

Whenever you are working under a van, make sure that it is properly supported. Always use axle stands, rated to at least two tonnes, and ensure that the vehicle is on a solid, level surface. When jacking the van, try to use the correct jacking points. These are located on the sills behind the front wheels and in front of the rear wheels.

Electrics

When you work on the electrics of your van, ensure that the vehicle battery earth is disconnected. Make sure that battery terminals, both on the vehicle and on the leisure battery, are covered in order to prevent short circuits. Be careful when working with batteries as battery acid is highly corrosive, and be sure to follow the manufacturer's instructions when using a battery charger. Failure to do so could result in the battery exploding or catching fire. Also be aware that certain circuits on a vehicle, such as the ignition system and starter wiring, carry very high levels of voltage and current; it is enough in some cases to cause a fatal electric shock.

When using mains power tools, ensure that they are plugged in via an RCD circuit breaker to protect against short circuits. It is surprisingly easy to chop through an electrical cable when not paying attention.

Fluids

Most of the fluids found in a vehicle, excluding perhaps the screen wash, can be harmful in one way or another, either to yourself or the environment. Oil is the most obvious of these. When changing the oil, be sure to catch it in a suitable container and make sure it is properly disposed of; most local recycling centres have the correct facilities. Be sure to wear rubber gloves when in contact with engine oil as it can cause skin problems.

Brake fluid can also be very harmful, so, again, wear gloves and catch it in a secure container. Additionally, brake fluid is what is known as hygroscopic, meaning that it absorbs moisture from the atmosphere. Over time, the fluid in your van will absorb moisture, which has the effect of lowering its boiling point. As a result, under hard or sustained braking, the fluid can boil, introducing air into the brake system and causing reduced braking efficiency. It is recommended that you have your fluid checked by a garage every year, and changed every 2–3 years, to keep your brakes working at their optimum level.

Never siphon fluids such as fuel or oil by mouth, as ingesting even a tiny amount can cause fatal health problems.

Fumes and Dust

When working on the vehicle, ensure that you take measures to reduce exposure to harmful fumes or dust. It may sound obvious, but you must only run the engine outside or in a very well-ventilated area to avoid carbon monoxide poisoning.

If painting with a spray gun or can, be sure to wear the correct type of mask, particularly if you are using certain paints that contain ingredients that can cause cancer or respiratory problems. When cutting materials, whether plastic, wood or metal, it is vital to wear a dust mask. It should be noted that the dust created when cutting painted metal panels can be very harmful.

Protective Gear

I have learnt the hard way that it always pays to wear the correct protective gear. When using a power tool such as a saw or a router, ensure that any safety guards are in place and wear eye protection. If using an angle grinder, wear a pair of heavy-duty gloves – a thin cutting disc will slice through skin and bone in milliseconds. Welding gauntlets are the best bet; they cannot completely protect you, but they will at least deflect a glancing blow. A good pair of mechanic's gloves will also help prevent skinned knuckles and cuts due to sharp edges.

Fire

There are plenty of jobs that have the potential to pose a fire risk. The last thing you want is for your pride and joy or, worse, your house, to go up in smoke. Always have a full powder or foam fire extinguisher to hand. Also, be aware of where sparks from operations such as grinding are landing; even small sparks can start a carpet smouldering, for example.

Mechanical Work

If you are at all unsure about your mechanical abilities, always get a trained professional to at least check your work. This applies to maintenance on the van's running gear and to areas such as gas and electrical installations. If you are not 100 per cent happy, get it checked.

3

chopping holes

ROOFS

A pop-top roof is one of the most worthwhile modifications you can make to your camper van. It will not be cheap, but the added space and flexibility that it will afford is unrivalled, and it will also add considerably to the resale value of your vehicle. Be warned: fitting a roof is not for the faint-hearted and involves a considerable amount of structural modification to the van. It is recommended that you undertake this work only if you are a confident DIY mechanic and have prior experience of working with vehicle structures. Although the actual work is not particularly difficult, if you do not have the correct information and skill, you could cause irreversible damage to your van. Do not be too intimidated, however; if you feel that a task of this magnitude is within your capabilities, read on and find out what it entails.

Roof Types

There are a variety of different pop-top roof variations available for the T5 and T4, with models to suit the budget and needs of most people. The key choice to make is whether you want a front-/rear-opening or side-opening roof – one hinges along the side of the van, while the other hinges at the rear or front. The majority of the roofs available are rear-hinging and they tend to be of a higher quality. It is also the case that very cheap offerings may not be as structurally sound, and might not follow the roofline as smoothly as more expensive versions.

It is possible to retro-fit a VW California roof, but this is a very involved process. When it comes to more basic aftermarket fitments, the top of the tree in terms of quality are those produced by a company called Reimo. This company has been producing camper conversion parts, from full interiors to roofs and awnings, since the early 1980s and their kit is top-notch. However, the quality comes at a price – their most basic pop-top will cost in the region of £3,000, without fitting. They offer a choice between front and rear lift versions as well as a range of high-top conversions, in case you prefer a fixed roof. Evidence of the quality of Reimo's designs is the fact that nearly every other roof on the market draws its inspiration from them.

If a Reimo roof is outside your budget, there are a number of other aftermarket suppliers. The price of such conversions ranges from £1,200 to £2,500 for DIY fitment, depending on the specification. For our conversion, a unit produced in-house by Cheshire Motor Caravans provided the best value/quality ratio available. Priced at £1,600 for a DIY fitment, the build quality of the unit is hard to fault. It is a rear-hinging design, with concertina rather than pivot hinges at the rear (meaning that the rear of the roof also rises by about 4in, or 20cm) and made from thick fibreglass.

The kit was supplied ready to fit, with the interior of the roof already carpet lined and with the roof fabric pre-attached. CMC also supplied all of the required reinforcing frames and sections as well as the vital measurements relating to where to cut and where to fix items such as the hinges and gas struts (which were also supplied). In summary, the kit consisted of the following:

- roof section, complete with gas struts, carpet lining, fabric and hinges;
- two side reinforcing channels and one front reinforcing frame;
- canvas tie-down strips; and
- two tie-down straps and eyelets.

Fitting: An Overview

As a brief overview, fitting a pop-top is an involved process, but not one that requires any highly specialized skill, simply an ability to measure correctly and cut accurately. It must also be remembered that removing a large section of the roof will reduce the structural stiffness of the van, hence the need for the addition of strengthening sections. To ensure that the stiffness is restored, careful attention needs to be paid to fitting and securing the supplied strengtheners to maintain structural integrity. If you are in any doubt about your ability to do this, get a professional conversion company to undertake the work.

Fitting: Stage 1 (Cutting)

Your first task prior to embarking on chopping the roof out is to give yourself as much space as possible. Removing the front seats will help considerably and, if you are adding a roof to an existing conversion, you may also want to pull out any interior units. If starting from scratch, it is best to fit

Remove the seats for access.

25

chopping holes

Seatbelt mounts need a 12-point spline bit.

Grab-handle screws.

Sun-visor clips are delicate.

Remove the cubbyhole.

the roof before completing any carpet lining. In the case of our project, however, time constraints and the lead time on the roof meant that the sides were carpeted prior to fitting the roof.

Next, the front and rear head liners are removed. The rear is attached in the same fashion as the side panels (*see* Chapter 4), but the front is a little more delicate and removal necessitates detaching a number of trim items. Start by unbolting the upper seatbelt mounts, using an M10 spline bit (note these are not the same as Torx bits). The grab handles above the doors are secured by two Phillips-head screws located behind small plastic covers. The sun visor clips are very delicate and easily broken, so the plastic covering must be prised off very carefully and the Phillips-head screws removed. The interior light fitting and the overhead cubby hole must also be removed.

Headlining will pull away.

Remove cables.

Pull away the B-pillar trim surrounds to release the head lining. It can then be gently pulled away from the front cab trim, and put away somewhere safe, to avoid damage.

Moving into the rear of the van, it is a good idea to detach the wiring that runs front to rear to prevent it being accidentally cut.

chopping holes

Protect van sides.

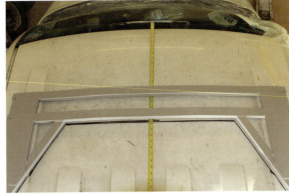
The reinforcement frame provides a reference for the front cut.

Mark cuts on the roof.

Mark with masking tape.

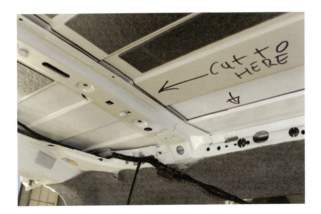
Mark internally.

Drill a starting hole.

Removing the roof skin will create a lot of metal chippings. To protect the bodywork, mask up the sides and front of the van using sheeting (remember to leave the tailgate free for access). Now you are ready for the most important stage: marking up where the cuts will be. These will vary from roof to roof, but, in the case of the unit supplied by CMC, the main cuts were in front of the rearmost roof reinforcing bar and along the inside edge of the first corrugation. The cuts were marked both internally and externally to avoid any disasters.

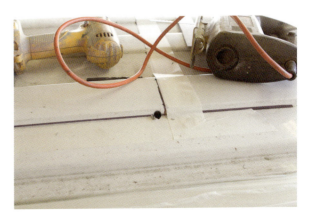
Enlarge the hole to accept a jigsaw.

chopping holes

The reinforcing section will provide lateral strength. Again, the exact measurements will vary from roof to roof, but in the case of the CMC unit a dimension was given from the top centre of the windscreen surround to the front edge of the reinforcement. The shape of the reinforcement can then be traced on to the roof, giving a clear cutting guide. A handy tip here is to mark the cut lines with masking tape. The reason for this is twofold. First, it makes it very clear where to cut; second, it protects the paint finish from undue scuffing during the cutting process. As with the windows, drill a guide hole from the inside of the van (where it is easy to see the reinforcing ribs) to double-check the location of the marked lines.

A reciprocating saw made light work of strengthening ribs.

Make sure you have a good working platform.

Once you are 100 per cent happy that your markings are in the correct place, it is time to start cutting. Make sure you have a solid platform from which to work. A pair of builder's trestles with planks or a folding step works well. It takes a while to make all of the cuts, so a comfortable working position is beneficial.

Begin by opening up the pilot hole with a large drill bit to allow a jigsaw blade to pass through. You will need a long metal-cutting blade in the saw; a reciprocating saw, which has a long stroke and cuts quickly, was used on this project. There are different schools of thought on how to go about cutting the skin out. Some favour cutting the main section into two halves to make it more manageable, but if you have assistance it can be removed in one piece. Try to keep the saw as vertical as possible – a tricky task, as the cut runs along the 'v' of the corrugations. Keep a tight grip on the saw as it will jump as it hits the strengthening bars below the surface.

Cut the sides then the front and the rear.

Padding will prevent you scalping yourself.

The main section removed.

Use a jigsaw for the front panel.

Securely fasten the frame in place.

Once you have cut out three of the sides of the panel, it helps to wedge a short length of timber underneath the flap to support it. You should be left with a neat hole in the top of the van. To prevent you scalping yourself, cover the sharp edge at the rear of the roof with some pipe lagging. With the bulk of the roof removed, access to the front section is much easier. A jigsaw is the best tool for this area as it is able to cut the tight corners more easily than the thicker-bladed reciprocating saw.

Ensure that the edges align.

The B-pillar top needed trimming to clear the frame.

Hopefully, if everything has gone to plan, you will have a gaping hole in the top of your van. If you are anything like me, you will probably be praying that it is in the right place, but there is no turning back now. The next task is to offer up the front reinforcing section. You may find that the roof requires a little extra trimming at this stage, particularly around the reinforcing plates at the top of the B-pillar.

Pop rivet at a maximum of 40mm intervals.

Once you are happy with the fit of the reinforcing frame, clamp it in place and mark out for drilling and riveting – every 40mm should be sufficient spacing. Both the front and rear of the frame will be riveted so measure from the edge of the cut to the middle of the frame on the underside of the roof and transpose the measurement to the top in order to mark the holes for the front section of the frame. To ensure maximum rigidity, use large pop rivets – our 4.8mm fixings required a 5mm hole to be drilled.

It is possible to do all of the riveting by hand, however, if you have access to a compressor, a pneumatic riveter saves a lot of effort. It is also possible to get a riveting attachment

chopping holes

for a cordless drill. If you must use a hand riveter, make sure it is the concertina/pliers type rather than a cheap single-handed tool – your arms will thank you for the investment.

work around the sliding door top rail. Simply trim it until it fits snugly.

Cut the roof bars to length.

Treat bare metal edges with zinc primer.

The door slider needs to be accommodated.

Paint the side panels if needed.

If the side rails were supplied in bare metal, give them a good coat of high-zinc primer to prevent any rust problems. The same applies to the cut edges of the roof. In order to keep over-spray to a minimum, use a small piece of cardboard to mask each section of roof as you spray.

Double-check the length of the opening.

Clamp in place and drill for rivets.

With the front frame firmly fixed in place, it is time to turn your attention to the side reinforcing rails. These are supplied un-cut, so you need to measure the exact distance from the front reinforcing section to the rear of the roof hole. Once you are sure you have the right measurements, trim the rails to length using a 1mm cutting disc on an angle grinder. You will find that the side rail will snag on the body-

chopping holes

High-strength bonding.

Ensure good adhesive coverage.

Rivet the underside of the strengtheners.

over. Do not worry that the roof still looks very industrial and unfinished. All of the metalwork you have just added will be covered in carpet later, giving it a factory-looking finish.

Get help lifting the roof on.

Hinge plates removed from the roof.

It is now time to trial-fit the roof, to check where it should line up. Make sure that you cover any sharp edges with masking tape. The roof used on this van came fully built up with the canvas already attached, so it was important to take care not to tear it before it was even fitted. The roof lifts up on a concertina hinge at the rear and is supported by gas struts at the front. The correct location of both the hinges and the struts is vital in ensuring the roof sits square both horizontally and longitudinally. CMC provided a measurement for the distance between the rear edge of the hinge mounting bracket and the back edge of the van. This may vary from roof type to roof type, for example, the Reimo roofs use one of the existing bolt holes provided by VW for roof-rack mounting. To make life easier, we removed the base plates from the hinges to mark up the holes, taking careful note of the orientation of all of the bolts and the arrangement of the hinge mechanism.

The roof came supplied with self-drilling fixings to secure the hinges, however, we preferred to use 'riv-nuts' (also known as Nutserts) instead. These work in a similar fashion to a pop rivet, but feature an internal thread that allows for a bolt to be screwed in. A special tool is needed to fit them; it will cost around £50, but it is a worthwhile investment as

Once the primer has dried, clamp the side rails in place and drill holes for rivets approximately every 100mm. Next, get a high-strength bonding agent and apply a liberal amount to the edges of the rails and the bodywork with which they will come into contact. This serves a dual purpose: it obviously helps secure the rails in place but it also helps keep moisture out of the joint. Once you are completely happy with the fitment, secure the rail in place with rivets along the upper and lower surface. Note: do not forget to feed any wiring back behind the reinforcing strips before you fix them in place!

You are now about half-way through the process and the intimidating phase of chopping, grinding and cutting is

chopping holes

A riv-nut fixing.

Check the operation of the hinge mechanism.

A riv-nut gun, much like a pop-riveter.

With the hinges reattached, you can check the elevation of the roof a couple of times, raising and lowering it, to ensure that it is sitting square on the roof. The hinge brackets are slotted, allowing for some movement to help align things. Reattaching all of the hinge mechanism can be a little tricky, requiring the roof to be raised. The roof is surprisingly heavy, so use a step ladder, or some other handy support, with a foam pad on top to hold the roof while you work. This takes the weight off your helper's arms, although you will still need someone on hand to keep everything steady.

it makes adding threaded inserts to panels a cinch. To fix the 'riv-nuts', drill a hole as you would for a pop rivet (ensuring that it is the correct size of course), then thread the nut on to the tool, insert in the hole and squeeze. The result is a perfect threaded fixing. Fixings are available in a variety of sizes and in both steel and aluminium. For this particular task, we used M6 coated steel inserts. With the hinge plates securely fixed, the rest of the mechanism may be reattached.

Secure the gas struts with self-drilling bolts.

A ladder with some foam makes a good 'third hand'.

Gas struts may need pressure releasing once fitted; be careful with this.

chopping holes

The roof is supported by a pair of gas struts, which were already fitted. The location of these struts is vital in ensuring that the roof raises and lowers correctly. CMC provided a measurement diagonally from the top centre of the screen to the side channel on the roof as the location for the front fixing screw of the strut. As it turned out, this tallied with one of VW's roof-rack fixing holes, making life easier. The struts come fully charged with gas, meaning they are locked in the out position and some pressure needs to be released to allow them to compress. This is achieved by turning a small Allen-head release screw on the strut body. Take it very gently, releasing a small amount of gas at a time until the roof can be pulled down on the attached grab handles. If you let too much gas out, the struts will not be able to support the weight of the roof.

Measure the width and length of the canvas with the roof pulled taut.

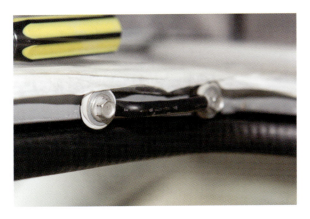

The tie-down fixing for the roof straps.

Cut and drill the fixing strips.

If your van is also your means of daily transport, at this stage you can secure the roof in place and drive it if necessary. The roof from CMC is clamped down at the front using a pair of tie-downs that run through eyelets on the front reinforcing frame and the roof. To fit these we first attached the fixings to the frame and then aligned the fixings on the roof. The roof was pilot-drilled from the underside, then drilled from the top to avoid cracking the gel-coat. The eyelets were then secured in place using bolts with sealing washers and a dab of sealant (be careful not to over-tighten these bolts, as this could cause cracking in the roof). With the straps in place the roof should be pretty much waterproof when closed, meaning you can drive the van if you need to, although it is preferable to complete the whole conversion in one go.

Fitting: Stage 2

Once you are happy that the roof is operating as it should and is located square on the van, it is time for probably the trickiest stage of the operation: securing the canvas. Cutting the hole for the roof may cause some anxiety, but it is actually quite straightforward; ensuring that the canvas fits well requires time and patience. Ultimately, you are aiming for a canvas that sits taut, with no wrinkles when the roof is elevated. While it will not severely affect the roof's functionality if the canvas is not completely smooth, it will make the van look shoddy from the outside. Given the amount of effort that goes into the conversion, this is not something you want.

Start from the middle and work outwards.

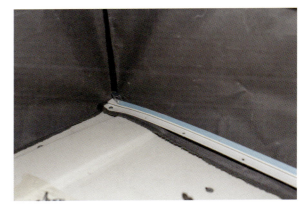

Try and avoid creases and wrinkles in the corners.

chopping holes

The first job is to figure out exactly where the canvas needs to sit to ensure that there are no bags or wrinkles on the side, then measure the distances between the corners. These will be the lengths to which you need to cut the securing strips. These can be trimmed to length using a pair of tin snips or a hacksaw. Once they have been cut, pre-drill holes every 100mm along the strips. Starting at the front edge, secure the strips using self-tapping screws, fixing the centre of the canvas first. A point to note here is that the strips have a slotted edge, which faces inwards and allows the carpet to be tucked neatly up to the edge of the roof. Be warned: the process of getting an even level of tautness around the roof can be a frustrating one, so work slowly and methodically until you are happy with the result.

Once you have fixed the front strip, attach the side and finally the back. It is much easier to take any slack up at the rear of the roof where any wrinkles are much less noticeable.

You want the canvas to look taut, with no wrinkles or creases.

If everything has gone to plan, you should end up with a tight canvas that will not flap about in the wind. The final task is to apply a bead of sealant around the outside edge of the canvas, at the joint with the van roof, to prevent any possible moisture ingress.

The gap between the side rails and the van body.

Make a cardboard template.

You are now nearly ready to carpet out the roof area, hiding all of the unsightly metalwork. However, there will be a void between the side reinforcing strips, the front frame and the pillar trims, which needs to be filled prior to carpeting. This may be done with a small piece of 5mm ply.

Mark the shape to be filled on to some thin ply.

Cut out the shape.

chopping holes

Fix the ply in place and blend in any sharp edges with sandpaper.

Start by making a cardboard template of the area to be filled. Transpose the template on to a sheet of ply and cut it out using a jigsaw. Fix it in place using some self-tapping screws. Note that the edge of the filler panel has been sanded to blend smoothly into the side reinforcement and tucked up under the front headliner. When wrapped, the carpet will return under the headliner and the pillar trim, providing an almost factory finish.

WINDOWS

Windows are not a necessity in a camper van, but they do make the whole camping experience less claustrophobic and, more importantly, completely transform the look of your vehicle. It would be fair to say that a window conversion is the single biggest, and probably best-value, alteration that you can make to the look of a T4 or 5. If you have started with a Caravelle or similar model that comes factory-fitted with side glass, you will be well aware that a glazed van looks much better than a panel variant. It may seem daunting at first glance, but if you are methodical it is well within the capabilities of the DIY converter to undertake the conversion. If you are not comfortable with undertaking the work yourself, there are a number of specialists who will do it for you for around £60 per window.

Our van still looks like a builder's van!

chopping holes

Window Options

In the past, window conversions on panel vans were fitted using rubber seals, which entailed a lot of hard work; today, nearly all the conversion kits on the market are fixed in place using a bonding adhesive in much the same way as modern car windscreens. Although using glue may sound like a less satisfactory solution than fixing with seals, the bonding agent used is an industry standard and provides a stronger and more weather-tight seal than any other method.

When choosing your glazing there are two real options: original VW and aftermarket. While it is always nice to use a genuine product, VW glass is considerably more expensive and the better aftermarket glass is of a perfectly good standard. It should also be considered that VW windows require more cutting to make them fit, so for a panel-van conversion aftermarket windows are probably a better option for the home installer. Just make sure that the glass is CE approved. The only other consideration is whether to use tinted or clear glass, with most suppliers offering both options. Tinted glass is definitely advantageous in a camper conversion. Not only does it offer some useful extra privacy, it can also help keep in-vehicle temperatures down in summer. If you do opt for tinted glass, make sure that the tinting is not simply a stick-on film as this can peel and discolour over time. If you use a reputable supplier such as CMC they will only sell proper 'privacy' glass.

Fitting: Stage 1 (Cutting)

You may also need to remove wheel-arch boxes.

The interior of the window panels.

The first job you will probably be faced with is removing any ply lining that is fitted to the inside of the van. Depending on how these were fitted, this may be easier said than done. For example, the panels may be riveted in place and the rivets will need drilling out. With any lining removed, you will be presented with internal frames in the shape of windows. Now for the daunting bit: cutting holes in your pristine van.

Clean the outside thoroughly.

Remove any ply lining.

chopping holes

Mark the corners.

Join up the pilot holes to indicate the area to cut.

Before doing any cutting, it is a good idea to give a thorough wipe-down to all of the surfaces around where you will be working. Ultimately the windows will be glued in, so cleanliness should be uppermost in your mind throughout the whole fitting process.

The cuts will need to follow the lines of the internal window apertures. If you are using a jigsaw, cutting will need to be undertaken from outside the van. This means that the internal lines are not visible, so you will need to draw guide lines to follow. Start by marking the corners of the internal curves. Take a small drill bit – 6mm will suffice – and drill guide holes in each of the four corners. These will provide a reference point on the outside skin for marking the cut lines. With all of the holes drilled, use a straight edge and permanent marker to join each point together; measure from the swage line to the line to ensure that they are in fact parallel. Use a round object to create the curved corner lines, first checking its profile against the inner curves and transposing this to the outside surface. A masking tape roll works well as a pattern.

Mask up the body to protect the paint.

Drill pilot holes.

Enlarge the pilot holes to accept a saw blade.

It is also important to protect the paintwork where you will be cutting. Apply several layers of masking tape to the panels around the window to stop the foot of the saw scratching the paint. The final step before cutting is to open out one of the guide holes so that it is large enough to accept a jigsaw blade.

chopping holes

Use a long metal cutting blade.

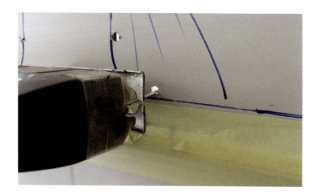
Start the jigsaw in a corner.

Carefully remove the cut panel, taking care, as the edges will be sharp.

Before beginning your cutting, make sure that the windows you plan to fit are stored securely out of the way – the last thing you want is for a window to get broken once you have chopped your van. Use a fine-toothed metal-cutting blade in the saw, to ensure a clean cut in the thin metal that forms the panel. Choose the longest blade you can find, because you will need to cut through the reinforcing struts in the centre of the window sections.

Slot the jigsaw into the enlarged guide hole and carefully cut along the line. It is wise to wear eye protection as the cuttings are sharp and hot. As you get towards the centre of the window, be prepared for the saw to kick back as you hit the reinforcing struts. It is difficult, but try and keep your cut line as close to the inner rolled edge as possible; once you have made the cut a few inches long, it is possible to bend the panel slightly so that you can see the inner edge.

Work from bottom to top, taking it very carefully on the corners. It is a good idea to have someone hold the bottom edge of the panel to stop it flapping as you cut out the top section. If everything has gone to plan – and you have not snapped all your saw blades – the panel can be lifted out, leaving you with a gaping hole in the side of your van.

Trim any excess with a grinder.

De-burr the edges.

Work from the bottom to top, and get someone to support the panel to stop it flapping.

You will now need to smooth off the sharp and ragged edge that is left on the remaining panel work. This can be done using a coarse-grit flap wheel on an angle grinder. The flap wheel can also be used to straighten any wonky edges and to get a smooth curve in the corners. To give the final finishing touch to the edges, use either a fine file or a cartridge roll on a die grinder to de-burr the inside edges of the panel. Having the inner edge completely smooth will help later on when it comes to fitting the carpet lining or rubber trims.

The final stage before starting to fix the windows in place is to spray etch primer on to the bare metal along the fresh cut. Moisture will inevitably gather in the joint, both from outside and inside the van (in the form of condensation), so the metal needs to be protected to prevent any rust issues.

Spray the joint between two windows matt black.

Window-fitting adhesive, and bonding agent.

Fitting: Stage 2

The fitting kit supplied by CMC consists of a tube of adhesive, a small pot of primer, an applicator for the primer and an alcohol wipe. Each kit provides enough material to fit one window.

Add a coat of zinc primer to prevent rust forming.

Wipe the frame with an alcohol wipe.

The holes ready to receive glass.

This is a neat trick of the trade suggested by Sam: when the windows are fitted, there is a small gap between the panes, which will stand out like a sore thumb. To counter this, mask up an oblong section where the windows meet and apply a coat of satin black paint. It is amazing how much small details like this can have a positive impact on the overall appearance of the job.

Apply the bonding agent.

chopping holes

As always, cleanliness is key. The strength of the glue relies on it being able to bond to the substrate, in this case the paint, and any dust, oil or other contamination will weaken the bond – cue your window popping out on the motorway. First, offer up the glass for a trial fit, so that you have an idea prior to gluing of where the panes will be located, then take the wipe from the window kit and thoroughly clean the edge of the window. Decant some of the primer into a small pot and apply it evenly to the metal surrounding the window aperture. The coat need only be a thin one, but it is important to ensure that all of the exposed metal is covered.

The window features a matte-black surround on its inside

Enlist a helping hand to place the window.

Repeat the process for the glass.

You have a couple of minutes to make adjustments.

Apply a thick bead of adhesive.

Fix in place with tape.

edge. This is another area where the glue will be applied, so any grease must be removed from here with the supplied wipe. Primer needs to be applied to the glass as well as the metal. Once primer has been applied to both surfaces, leave them for 10–15 minutes for the coating to flash off.

You are now ready to get gluing. A handy hint is to place the tubes of adhesive in hot water for 10 minutes, which will have the effect of softening the glue, making it a lot easier to squeeze from the tube. Apply an even bead around the entire window, keeping well away from the clear section of glass; the glue will be squeezed out when you fit the window and you do not want any showing.

When it comes to fitting the glass, it is a good idea to get

some assistance – dropping the window would not be good at this stage. Once the glass is in place, you have a short time to make any adjustments before the adhesive goes off. Make sure that the gap between the window recess and the glass is equal all round. A point to note is that, with the sliding window, an optical illusion makes it look like the window is not straight; trust the line between the window edge and the recess as your reference point. The final stage is to secure the glass with a few strips of masking tape. It should not slip but it never hurts to take precautions.

If you have followed these stages correctly you should

No longer a builder's van!

now be the proud owner of a fully glazed van. The adhesive is supposed to dry sufficiently quickly to allow you to drive away in an hour, but leave it as long as you can to go off.

Once all the windows are fitted, give the van a good soaking with a hose to check for any leaks.

4

ground work

INSULATION AND SOUND-DEADENING

If you are planning to use your camper van at all in inclement weather, keeping warm will be an important concern. Ultimately, a van is just a steel box and, with steel being a good conductor of heat, if it is left as standard it will cool down and heat up very quickly. Fortunately, there is a host of options when it comes to ensuring a pleasant climate inside your camper. All of these work on the basis of reducing the thermal conductivity of the vehicle, ensuring the warm air inside stays warm by reducing heat transfer to the cool outside air.

On top of thermal insulation, you also need to consider noise insulation, both when driving and when camping. A bare van is a noisy place to be when driving; it was designed as a working vehicle after all and the sound-deadening of the panels is almost non-existent. The same applies when the van is parked up, so retro-fitting of some form of sound-deadening will be vital if you want to improve your levels of comfort.

Both insulation and sound-deadening are generally fitted in the same parts of the vehicle and there are a number of options and dual-use materials on the market that fulfil both roles.

Materials

The purpose of insulation is to reduce the level of thermal conductivity from inside your van to the outside. In principle this is achieved in exactly the same way as with a house: layers of material are placed between the inner and outer walls to try and keep the heat in. There are a number of routes you can take to achieve this, all of which involve placing material in the side cavities of the van between the steel panels and the interior lining. One popular material for this is Celotex, a foil-backed foam that is used extensively in the building trade and is available in a variety of different thicknesses. It is easily cut to shape and can be wedged in the cavities to provide a good level of insulation. Another option is flash band, which is also used in the building industry; this material is supplied on a roll and, although it is not cheap, it is easy to fit and again provides excellent insulation properties.

Insulation (light) and carpet lining.

Insulation feels much like carpet but is made from a different material.

For those conscious about the environmental impact of their activities, a company called Amdro supplies a range of more traditional materials based on sheep's wool. This has been used for generations and has seen a resurgence in popularity in recent years as an eco-friendly and effective means of insulation.

For our project another fibre-based material was chosen, and supplied by Cheshire Motors Caravans, to provide both insulation and sound-deadening. It is an engineered felt, very similar to that used by many vehicle manufacturers in production vehicles. Supplied on a roll, it should provide good insulation on all but the coldest nights. It should also reduce vibrations in the body panels – a significant contributory factor to overall interior noise levels when driving.

Fitting

Trim panels must be removed.

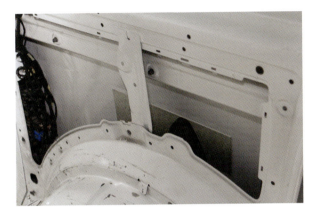

The voids behind the trim panels.

The sound-deadening/insulation is fitted behind the interior panels, so the first job is to remove these. They are secured with threaded pop-in fasteners, which can be a pain to remove, because it is very easy to round off the Allen key socket in them. To counter this, the best tool for the job seems to be an imperial-sized Allen key. This needs a little more force to push in, but is less likely to slip.

Remove fixings with an Allen key, taking care, as they are very fragile.

With the panel removed it is possible to access the outer skin of the vehicle. There may already be a section of factory-fitted sound-deadening material affixed to the body. You are going to need to glue to this surface, so it should be given a thorough clean with solvent cleaner.

High-temperature adhesive from CMC.

THE ADHESIVE

The contact adhesive supplied by CMC is specifically for high-temperature applications. There is a good reason for this: on a hot day the outer skin of the van can get very hot, which can cause adhesives of a lesser quality to come unstuck. You do not want your carpet lining to peel off on to your head when you are out on a summer trip! To work correctly, the glue needs to be sprayed on both surfaces that are being stuck. Be careful though; it can go everywhere!

Use the panels as a guide for cutting the material.

ground work

Use sharp scissors or a carpet knife.

Refit the trim panels.

Coat both the panel and the deadening with adhesive.

Once the glue is tacky, simply place the material up against the panel, shaping it to the various contours and curves. Where there are strengthening ribs, use a sharp knife to slit the material to allow it to conform more closely to the panel shape. With all of the panels deadened, place the covers back in place and reinsert the pop screws.

Do not forget about the small panels in the pillars.

You want to put insulation behind all of the panels, which will double neatly as templates. The material does not have to be cut perfectly to shape so do not worry too much about accuracy. Use a sharp pair of scissors or a knife to cut the material. The space behind the panels is obviously larger than the panels themselves so, to maximize the amount of insulation, add a few extra inches to the piece you are cutting. Coat both the panel and the material with an even coating of the spray glue. One can should suffice for affixing all of the sound-deadening you need. Leave the glue for a couple of minutes until it is dry to the touch.

One last note on the sound-deadening front: do not forget about the small panels by the sliding door – every little helps.

CARPET LINING

Cover the panel with the deadening, working it into the contours.

Mask up anything that you want to protect from glue.

ground work

With the interior all snug and warm it is time to add some carpet. This looks very similar to the insulation, but is much more stretchy, allowing it conform to the contours of the panels.

Apply contact adhesive to the surfaces to be carpeted.

Get a helper to assist with carrying the carpet into the van.

Start working the carpet in from the corners.

A pair of scissors works well to push the material into recesses.

Do the same for the carpet.

First, mask up anything you do not want to get glue on, then coat all of the areas that are going to be carpeted with an even layer of adhesive. Do the same for the carpet. Ours was supplied pre-cut in sections for each side of the van and a roof; if yours is not, simply measure the van sides roughly and then trim it to fit once it is in place.

At this stage, it is really useful to have someone to help. Move the glued sheet into the van, taking care not to let it get stuck on the way. Starting at the top, begin to work the carpet around the contours while ensuring that there are no wrinkles or creases forming. A pair of scissors is ideal for smoothing the carpet into the curves around the window frames and other tight spots.

ground work

Trim around the arches.

Tuck the flap under the seal.

The wheel arches can be a bit tricky, but some careful cutting will allow the carpet to smoothly form around the curve. Trim the carpet up to the return lip of the arch and then use a separate piece to cover the wheel well itself.

Use a flat implement to work the material under the pillar trims.

Cut a cross in the carpet covering the windows.

A top tip from Sam Jeffery is to make diagonal cuts out from the centre of each window. This makes it a lot easier to push the carpet into the corners. Use a similar approach at the front of the van, using a flat blade to push the carpet behind the pillar trim.

Work the material in around the window frames.

Leave about an inch spare around the tailgate seal.

When it comes to the rear door, trim the carpet so that it sticks past the rear seal by about an inch (25mm); it can then simply be flipped under the seal, providing a neat finish. The carpet around the front-door pillars can be treated in a similar fashion, with the carpet being tucked under the trim panels once it is trimmed down. The glue used to fit the windows means that they sit just far enough from the side panels to allow the carpet to be tucked between the glass and the metal. You can use rubber finishing strips here, but the carpet itself will provide a pretty neat solution.

ground work

Coat the wheel arches with adhesive.

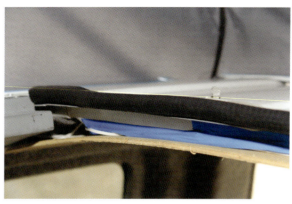
Rubber trim around the roof edge.

Cut a suitable size section to cover the arch.

Mark out the sections on a single piece of carpet.

Mould and stretch the carpet to shape around the wheel arch, then trim off the excess.

If you have a pop-top roof fitted, the area of exposed van roof also needs to be trimmed. To start with, a method is needed to cover the sharp edge at the rear of the roof. We used a spare section of the rubber trim that had been used to finish the area of headlining at the front of the cab. You then need to measure up each area of the roof and mark out the sections on the piece of carpet you plan to use. To make life easier, the carpet will be fitted in four sections, one front and back and one on each side.

In order to cover the wheel arches, mask off the areas that you have already carpeted and cut a section of carpet that covers the arch. Coat both the metalwork and the carpet with glue and drape the carpet over the arch. With some judicious stretching and the careful use of a pair of scissors, the carpet should mould neatly to the shape. Use sharp scissors to trim off any excess.

Start with the side sections.

ground work

Slits are cut to accommodate lights.

Fit the front section as a square and trim to fit.

With the carpet cut to size, repeat the process of applying glue to both the van and the carpet that you used for the main interior. Take special care not to get any glue on the pop-top fabric. The plastic strips that retain the fabric of the roof have a slot incorporated under which the carpet can be neatly tucked. Leave the joint where the roof carpet and the interior carpet meet loose for the moment; once everything is finished, this can be trimmed straight. If you want to run the wiring for the interior lights under the carpet, cut small slits for this purpose.

Fit the rear section on, starting at the back edge of the roof (see here from the pop top).

Smooth the rear section of carpet to the roof contours.

With the sides in place, fit the rearmost section of carpet. In this van, it extended from the tailgate seal to the back of the roof fabric so it was important to ensure sufficient material was used to cover all of the surfaces. As with the wheel arches, you need to use a combination of stretching and moulding with a pair of scissors to get the carpet to conform to all of the contours.

The final part to be fitted is the front section. This starts out as a square, with the centre section trimmed out once the edges are stuck in place. The carpet is returned under the roof reinforcing frame between the headlining and the steel structure, creating a very neat finished edge.

FLOORING

Unless you have purchased a Caravelle or similar, your van will probably feature either a plain steel floor or will have been lined with a protective layer of plywood. It may seem like stating the obvious, but the floor will form the foundation of any interior you are planning and thus it pays to ensure it is up to the task. Generally speaking, the floor of a camper will consist of three components: an insulating layer, a solid substrate and a covering.

For our project, the decision was made to keep things simple, but this is by no means a definitive approach. You may well feel that there are areas that can be improved or modified to suit your own needs. In terms of insulation, many of the materials used on the side panels of a van can also be utilized for the floor, but the area to be covered is extensive and this can add significantly to the overall build costs.

There is always the option not to add any form of insulation but, with both comfort and budget in mind, we came up with a low-cost and, hopefully, effective solution. This consists of budget-priced foam camping mats with a foil coating, which should perform a similar role to purpose-made insulation, but at a fraction of the cost. Four mats, sufficient to cover the entire floor area, came to less than £20. On top of this was placed a layer of 12mm marine plywood, cut to the shape of the floor, which was in turn covered by a layer of Altro Contrax flooring, a heavy-duty industrial covering with a non-slip coating. The choice of floor covering is a subjective one, and you can use anything from carpet to tongue and groove. For this project, the hard-wearing nature of the Altro covering was considered to be worth the extra investment over cheaper alternatives. It was also conveniently available from an online retailer pre-cut to fit the floor of a T5. As will become apparent later, this simplified considerably the process of constructing the floor.

Remove any flooring already in place.

The first task is to remove any existing floor covering and clean the load-bed area. With the ply lining of the van removed, ten years' worth of accumulated sand and gravel filling the channels were revealed. This took several hours to remove, but it is imperative that the bed is as clean and dry as possible, both to limit the potential for moisture build-up and to provide the best possible surface for glue to stick to.

After some solid cleaning the van is ready for its new flooring.

Fit filler strips in floor recesses.

With the floor clean, lay out the pre-cut flooring to check for fit. Ours was very close – so close, indeed that it would need some slight trimming to clear the carpet lining. It is important to ensure that the flooring is accurately shaped as it will be used as a template for the plywood. There should be as little movement as possible in the final floor. Although 12mm ply is pretty tough, it can still flex, which will cause no end of creaks and rattles. To combat this, sections of 9mm plywood packers need to be affixed in the larger gaps between the floor ridges. Not only will this prevent the upper layer of ply bending, it will also provide a good location for fixing the floor down. Remove the load-securing eyelets. The bolt holes for these will be used later in the conversion, primarily for securing the bed, so it is important that they remain accessible through the floor. Mark their position and drill a 10–15mm hole in the packers that sit over them. Secure the packers in place using a strong adhesive such as Grip Fill.

The pre-cut flooring makes a good template for the ply.

Tape the template down to stop it slipping.

ground work

Add an extra quarter of an inch (5mm) when cutting.

The step inserts will probably need extra trimming too.

It is now time to use the floor covering as a template for the main plywood sections. The back of a T5 is just over 4ft wide, so a regular 8ft × 4ft sheet of ply is not sufficient to create a complete floor. Two sheets will be required. If you have space, lay out the two pieces of ply and place the covering on top. Mark around the edges, then draw a second line about a quarter of an inch (5mm) inside the original line. This will provide sufficient clearance for the carpet lining while not leaving an unsightly gap.

Using a jigsaw, carefully cut around the marks you have made, trying to keep the edges as straight as possible (which can be difficult with a jigsaw). Once the sections are cut, offer them up to the inside of the van. There will be areas where they do not fit perfectly. This is due to the fact that some parts, such as the door pillar, taper downwards. It becomes a process of trial and error to get a perfect fit – trimming a small amount at a time from the areas in question until you achieve this.

To accommodate the extra depth of the flooring, you will need to use a deeper side step from a Caravelle or similar. These can be purchased from most parts suppliers or direct from VW. Some trimming of the ply may be necessary to ensure that the step fits snugly in place.

Carefully cut with a jigsaw.

Cheap insulation provided by sleeping mats.

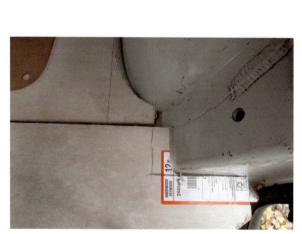
Door pillars will probably need extra trimming.

Trim the under-floor insulation to fit as closely as possible.

ground work

A sharp knife will remove any excess.

Once you are totally happy with the fit and finish of the plywood, it is a good idea to place some insulation under the flooring. It may seem like overkill, but it will make a considerable difference on a chilly night. There are many different insulation materials available, but the cheap foil-backed foam mats seemed like the ideal solution. The material cuts easily to the floor shape and once trimmed it can be simply glued in place using contact adhesive.

Holes drilled for access to load bolts.

Solid flooring.

The next stage is optional, but we decided it would be useful to be able to access the load-bay securing eyelets if necessary. To achieve this, the locations of the bolt holes were marked and a hole saw used to cut away the wood. The holes will be covered up by the vinyl flooring but this can be easily trimmed away in future if needed.

With the wood flooring fitting snugly, all that is left to do is to secure it in place with plenty of wood screws. These only need to be screwed into the pre-glued ply strips underneath, so that the metal floor of the van is not penetrated. Pay particular attention to the joint between the two sections of flooring as this needs to be dead flush to prevent a lip forming in the floor covering. Make sure that the floor is securely attached as any movement will lead to annoying creaks while driving.

Place the flooring in and glue it if desired.

The floor may need trimming to fit around the carpet.

The final job is to lay the floor covering in place. Ours was indeed an exact fit, as the supplier had promised; in fact, it needed trimming in order to accommodate the extra thickness of the carpet lining. This flooring is very tough, so use a decent-quality hooked knife blade to fettle it. You can then either glue the floor in place or simply leave it loose (which we decided to do). It is pretty rigid and not gluing it will make it easier should the covering ever need to be removed.

5
making a box a home

Hopefully, by this point in your conversion, you will have a pretty good idea of how you want the interior of your van to be laid out. This chapter can be used in two ways. First, you can simply copy our plans exactly and build a fully functioning set of storage units using the same appliances, or you can use the information to customize the features to suit your taste.

MATERIALS

The materials you use to build your storage units will inevitably dictate the level of finish you achieve. If you use cheap materials, ultimately, the interior will not last as well or look as good as if you use more expensive, higher-quality ones. The flip side to this is that it is more costly if you mess something up. Fortunately, there is a wide range of materials available.

MDF

Medium-density fibreboard (MDF) is the favourite of DIY enthusiasts, thanks in part to the efforts of all those home-improvement TV shows. It is an engineered wood product made by breaking down hardwood or softwood waste into wood fibres, often in a defibrator, combining it with wax and a resin binder, and then forming panels by applying high temperatures and pressure. The benefits of MDF are that it is cheap, easy to work with and has a smooth surface finish. The downsides are that it is very dense and, unless properly sealed, very susceptible to water damage.

As an additional consideration, it should be noted that, while it is always good practice to use a face mask when cutting materials, it is especially important with MDF. The dust is very fine and inhaling it can cause respiratory problems.

Furniture Board/Melamine

If you have ever purchased any flat-pack furniture, it is more than likely that it will have been made from furniture board, often called Melamine. Melamine is made from chipboard – board made, as it names suggests, from glued and compressed wood chips – covered in a layer of veneer. A huge range of surface finishes is available and the board is easy to cut and shape. Stick-on edging strips are used to finish cut edges. The key advantage of these boards is that they are cheap and have a high-quality surface finish. However, as is the case with MDF, the boards are heavy and disintegrate if moisture gets under the veneer.

Soft and Hardwood Ply (Builders' Ply)

Plywood, made from lots of thin sheets of wood glued together, is available in many different versions, from low-quality 'shuttering ply' through to beautifully finished materials intended for furniture construction. For making furniture units, the minimum quality you want to consider is what is known as 'WBP', or marine plywood. Most DIY stores and timber merchants will stock this type of wood, which is laminated using a 'water- and boil-proof' glue and uses hardwood for the plies. This makes it very durable and resistant to moisture. The high quality of the wood also means that it sands well, producing a fine finish for either painting or varnishing.

Furniture ply is available in a host of finishes.

making a box a home

Lightweight Ply

The key material requirements for a camper interior are a high-quality finish and lightweight. Given the size of the camper and motorhome market, it should come as no surprise that there are a number of companies that have developed bespoke products for reapplications in that market. These materials are generally referred to as lightweight furniture ply; Vohringer is probably one of the best-known suppliers. The boards consist of a lightweight ply core covered in a thin surface veneer. They are available in a plethora of different finishes and textures, from traditional wood grains to bright primary colours and even effects such as carbon fibre and brushed stainless steel. If you take your van to a reputable conversion company, they will invariably use this type of wood, and it is the industry standard for caravans and motorhomes. The cut edges do show the interior plies, so knock-on edging strips are generally used to provide a tidy finish.

The one disadvantage of this material is cost. A 2,400 × 1,200mm sheet will set you back at least double the price of a similar sheet of WBP and probably four times that of MDF. However, it is the only material that provides an excellent finish and good durability, without doubling the weight of your van. These were the benefits that led us to choose it for our project.

THE UNITS

Plans

These plans (*see* below) are for a basic kitchen and cupboard installation in a T5 van. With some tweaking around the wheel arches, these units will also happily fit in a T4. Make sure you read this whole chapter before embarking on building these units (unless you are already an experienced cabinet-maker or similar). There are a number of methods used and checks to undertake in order to make life easier and ensure everything fits where it should.

An initial design for the interior.

making a box a home

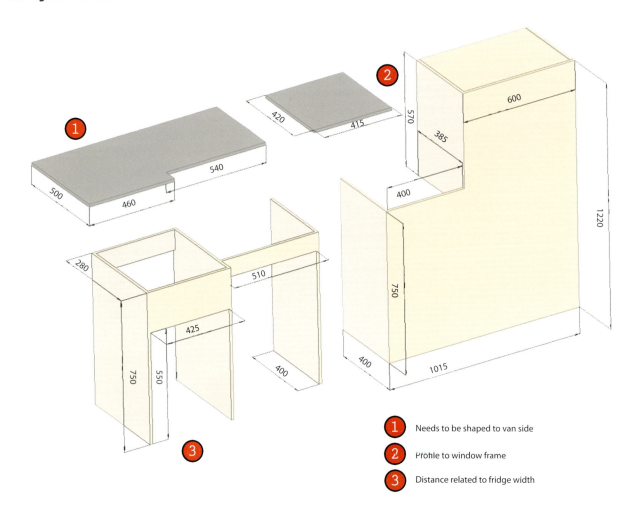

Plans for basic T5 interior units.

VWorks produces a bespoke interior for every particular van that it works on, and the design for our T5 was no different. Although Sam Jeffery has years of experience working with a well-known conversion specialist, the design for our van was something of a prototype. The intention was that it should be as simple as possible for the home builder to construct, provided they were to take sufficient time and care. For this reason, some of the fancier features, such as curved surfaces and complex profiles, have been omitted. It was also designed with an eye towards budget; for example, we eschewed the use of an expensive fitted water tank in favour of a basic jerry can. It may take up a bit of interior space, but that decision saved around £100. Additionally, the units were designed to use as little material as possible; it should be feasible to construct this interior using three 1,200 × 2,400mm sheets of wood – two for the cupboards and bed facia and one for the worktop.

> **TOOL SAFETY**
>
> The tools you will use to build the interior units have to ability to cause serious injury. With saws and routers, *always* make sure any guards are in place and *always* wear eye protection. Also be aware that the glue used to make plywood can be harmful, so it is best to wear a face mask when cutting.
>
> It is not unheard of for a DIYer to chop though the electrical flexes on tools, so make sure that you have an RCD fitted to any plugs you are using. You will also be drilling into and through the body of the van, so always check that there are no pipes or hoses on the other side of any panels. Also, check that you are not about to drill through the outside skin of the van!
> You will need the following tools:
>
> - jigsaw;
> - circular saw;
> - router and 3mm slotting cutter;
> - hole saw;
> - drill/driver;
> - 6 × 1 self-tapping screws; and
> - basic hand tools.

Construction

Once you have decided on the layout of your van, it is time to start building, however you must resist the temptation to dive in too quickly. For a start, the lightweight furniture ply is not cheap, so you must avoid any waste.

Before you start working, ensure that you have a good clear area where you can lay out a full sheet of timber. A good solution for a collapsible working table is a pair of trestles (available at most DIY/builders' merchants) with a sheet of 22mm ply or MDF on top. Not everyone has access to a large covered workshop, so if you are doing the conversion work on your drive, clear out the garage and set it up as a temporary workshop. The last thing you want to have happen is for the heavens to open and the materials to be ruined.

Make careful notes.

Measure the height from the floor to the windows.

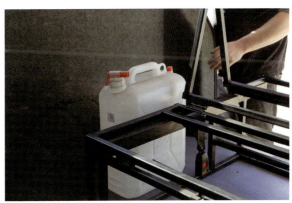

Checking the clearance between the bed and the arch with a water container fitted.

Measure the height of the rear headlining.

Clear ample working space.

Even if you are using our design drawings, it is worth measuring out the exact dimensions of your van's interior. Different combinations of flooring, carpet and insulation could mean that certain parts need trimming or adjusting to obtain a correct fit. The most important measurements are those from the floor to the base of the windows, to the roof at the rear of the van, and from the side of the bed to the wheel arch. Double-check that a standard water container will fit between the wheel arch and the bed, taking into account clearance for the bed to move and 15mm for the timber thickness.

making a box a home

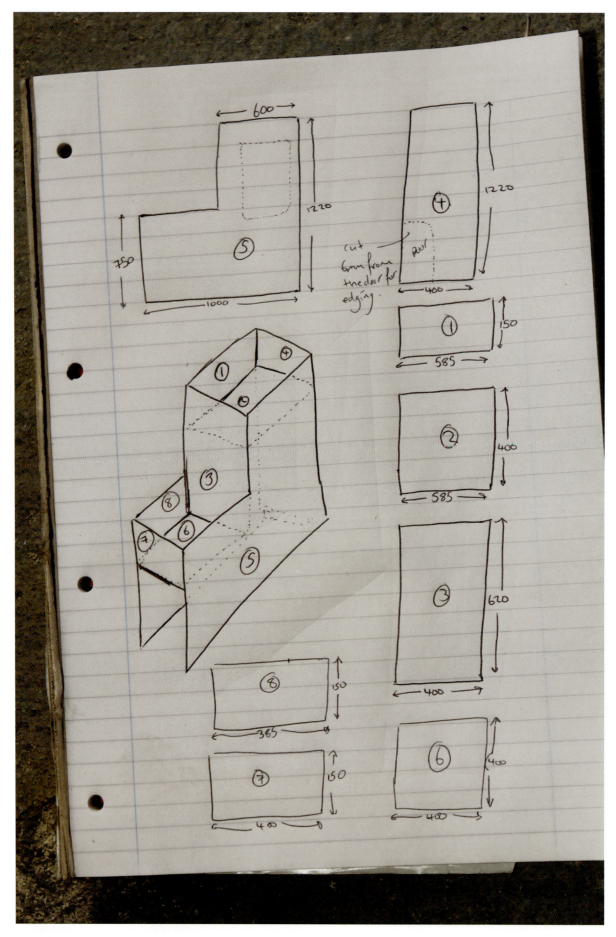

It is a good idea to sketch your final plans and dimensions.

Sam's initial plans for the rear cupboard unit show that it does not reach the roof of the van, for the very good reason that it is 1200mm tall, or the width of a sheet. A full-height cupboard would have entailed the use of another full sheet of timber, adding more cost to the build. Note that each panel is numbered; the numbers can then be added to the actual panels as they are cut, making it much easier to keep track of the component parts. After all, one piece of wood looks very similar to another and you do not want to chop up your wardrobe top cover inadvertently, thinking it is an off-cut.

Start marking up your wood.

A large metal angle makes an excellent straight edge.

The first section to be cut was the side of the wardrobe, no.5 on the plan. If you do not have a long ruler, a tape measure and a straight length of timber or metal angle will suffice. The long straight cuts for this panel were made with a circular saw. A handy tip here is to use a piece of metal angle as a guide. Mark out your cut line, add the width of the saw's fence and the blade, then mark a second line. Clamp the angle along this line and use it to guide the saw, ensuring a nice straight cut.

Create a cardboard template for the rear panel.

You will also need a cardboard template for the front panel.

Make sure it the template is a good fit around the window frame profile.

Next, we offered up the wardrobe side panel in order to work out the profile of the rear panel. Use a large piece of cardboard to make a template; draw the curve of the van side by eye, and then trim it to fit exactly. Repeat the process for the front of the cupboard, noting that the side windows slope inwards towards the top.

Once you are happy with the templates, mark out the profiles on the plywood then cut the edge using a jigsaw. Note: if you are using wood veneer sheets, check the direction of the grain. It looks a little strange if the grain on the side panel runs horizontally while that on the end panels runs vertically. The hole for the door on the rear panel can also be cut at this stage. It will be a flush-fitting door, with edge trimming on both the door and the hole, so you need to leave about 6mm of clearance to account for the edging. A roll of masking tape makes an ideal template for the curved corners; if you use the same roll (without using any of the tape) for the whole interior, all of your curves will have the same radius. At the same time, you can cut the aperture for the tambour door (*see* page 59 for advice on the fitting of this).

Transfer the template to the wood.

Test-fitting the wardrobe unit.

The finished panel should be a tight fit to the bodywork.

A masking tape roll makes an excellent corner template.

Small fixing blocks secure the panels together.

making a box a home

All of the sections ready for assembly.

Checking for size against the fridge.

Check everything fits before screwing in place.

Ensure that the seat will not interfere with the units.

With the side, front and rear panels sorted, we then proceeded to cut the various infill panels shown in the earlier sketch. To ensure that they would be exactly the right size, we fixed the panels we had cut in place using simple plastic cupboard fixings. These may not be as pretty as dovetail joints, but they are very quick and easy and make aligning the panels simple. Once we had double-checked all of the measurements, it was time to cut the various panels. The whole unit was then assembled out of the van, making it much easier to access the various fixings, before being placed back in the van. As this cupboard was going to act as the reference point for the front units, we fixed it in place with a couple of screws to prevent any measuring inconsistencies.

Checking sink clearance.

The dimensions of the front units are dictated by the type and size of appliances you have chosen as well as the proximity of the front seat. To start with we positioned the fridge in the desired location and pushed the driver's seat back to its furthest extent to check clearance. Happy that everything was in the correct place we cut a pair of dividing panels to the same height as the rear cupboard and the depth of the fridge, and a rear panel to fix to the wardrobe unit (this needs to be profiled to the wheel arch). Once these were cut, it became clear that there was sufficient clearance to mount the sink above the fridge. (Initially we were not sure this would be the case as the sink is deeper than the cooker.)

TAMBOUR DOORS

Roller shutter or tambour doors are a brilliant idea in a camper van, where space is at a premium. Using a normal-opening regular door on the wardrobe in our van would have been impractical, due to the proximity of the bed. Rather than using a very small door, or a large door that could only be opened with the bed laid flat, a roller door would allow access regardless of the bed position. Doors of this type are readily available from a number of camping interior suppliers, with a range of finishes. Gallant (gallantuk.com) supplied one to our exact measurements, with a silver finish to match the edge trimming, for around £60. These doors look very smart, but they are actually very simple to fit.

Drill a central fixing hole.

A tambour door set.

Countersink track-securing screws.

Support brackets for the door tracks.

Check that the door slides smoothly.

The 500 x 400mm door was supplied with two cassettes into which it would roll, a pair of guide tracks and the roller itself. The tracks and cassettes need to be mounted on plates – simple sections of wood – to give them rigidity. Instead of using separate plates, it is possible to connect the tracks directly to the top and bottom plates of the wardrobe cupboard. However, we wanted the cupboard to extend below the level of the door. Fixing holes were carefully drilled in the plastic parts, adding a countersink to prevent the fixing screws from sitting proud. Once the plates were complete, the door was test-fitted in the runners to check that everything moved smoothly and the door would not snag on the fixing screws.

The assembled door was laid out on the wardrobe side panel to work out exactly where it needed fixing. We added a cross piece to join the two tracks, to help keep everything square. This was cut to a length such that there was a small amount of free play between the door and the shutter, allowing it to slide smoothly. It was decided that the front of the door would sit as close to the edge of the cupboard as possible, meaning that the distance between the edge of the panel and the door frame was 15mm, to take account of the front panel. A small off-cut of ply was used to gauge the distance needed.

Assembling the door on the wardrobe panel.

Mark and cut the door aperture.

Remember to leave clearance for other panels.

Fix the door in place.

Once we were happy with the location of the door frame, it was time to cut the opening, using the trusty masking tape roll to radius the corners. The aperture was cut using a jigsaw. Once the hole was cut, the edging strip was fitted and some holes were carefully countersunk through the edge of the frame. This was then screwed to the wardrobe panel, taking care not to break through the outer skin. With the rest of the cupboard reassembled, this method should produce a very neat and professional-looking tambour door.

KNOCK-ON EDGING

Knock-on edge trim.

Knock-on edging is available in a number of different colours; we chose silver to go with the light fittings and tambour door. For fitting, you need to cut a slot around the outside edge of the board, using a 3mm slotting bit in a router. First, set the router bit so that it is exactly central on the board. Clamp the board to your work surface and carefully machine the slot. Be careful not to leave the router in the same place for too long, as this can cause the wood to scorch. If you have not used a router before, practise on some off-cuts first to get a feel for it.

A knock-on edge strip will give a neat finish where the edge of the boards will be showing. You can get iron-on edging, but it is easy to chip and can be very awkward to fit. This sort of edging is likely to be found only on a mass-produced interior, such as those found in a Bilbo's van, where the boards are CNC cut at the factory and the edge is applied by machine.

Use a rubber mallet to knock the edging into place; wrap the head in tape to prevent marking.

With the slots cut, simply tap the edging in using a rubber mallet with some masking tape wrapped around the end so that it does not mark. If it is very cold, you may find the edging is stiff, so gently warm it with a hot-air gun first.

Rout a 3mm slot in the panel.

This will be the cooker and cupboard area.

Things are starting to come together.

making a box a home

Cut a small V to help the edging conform to the corners.

Stretch and tap the edging into place.

Gently heat the edging to aid flexibility.

When it comes to tight corners, the inner edge of the material needs to be notched slightly to allow it to conform to the shape. Simply use a sharp knife to cut a small V in the edging. To make sure you get a close fit, heat the edging (carefully, so as not to burn it) and tap it into place while gently pulling the loose end tight.

Leave a small amount of excess to account for shrinkage over time.

When you get to the join in the edging, leave it a few millimetres over length, tuck it in and then hammer it home. Over time the edging can shrink but, as long as a bit of extra material is left in place, you should not end up with a gap.

Angle brackets secure the units to the van.

The gap left will house a storage cupboard and drawer. Note that the top edge of the front panel on the wardrobe (highlighted) has been edged as this will be visible when the top of the storage area next to it is opened. The edging on the vertical end panel of the wardrobe has a lip on both sides, and thus will cover the joint between the front and rear units. It is then a case of cutting out the infill panels, including the shelf that will sit below the cooker. Once these are fixed in place, the basic structure of the interior units is complete and your van will be starting to look like a camper. The final task before you can start work on the top sheet is to check that the front and rear sections align properly, and add a couple of fixings to keep everything in place. Basic right-angle brackets are ideal for this, allowing you to fix the units to the bodywork using self-tapping screws.

making a box a home

Measure up for the worktop.

Place the worktop on the units and scribe around it.

The worktop starts out as an oblong.

Once the rectangle is cut, offer it up to the unit. You will find that the wall of the van tapers front to rear, meaning that you will need to cut a corresponding taper on the worktop. Once you have done this, the back right-hand corner of the panel will also need profiling, to match the curve of the window pillar. As with the previous profiles, judge the cut by eye and remove a small amount of material at a time until the top fits snugly.

Rounded corners prevent accidents.

WORKTOP AND APPLIANCES

With everything aligned and square, measure up the worktop. This will extend out slightly from the front of the cupboards, much as you would find with a normal kitchen worktop. Once again, the measurements shown on our plans are a guide only – slight variations between your measuring and ours may mean the size needs to be adjusted a little. Start by cutting the worktop out as a simple rectangle. We chose a brushed stainless-steel veneer finish to suit the theme of the van, but there is a host of other veneers available.

Some extra clearance was needed for the window surround.

Profile the back edge to conform to the van side.

If you are happy with the alignment of the top, it is time to turn your attention to the front edge. While there would be nothing wrong with leaving it all square, nice rounded edges are much more pleasing to the eye (and less painful to bump into). Place the worktop on the base units, ensuring that it is in the correct position, and mark around the underside of the board. This should leave you with a clear line showing the edge of the cupboards. Remove the worktop and place it bottom side up on your work bench. Now mark a line 10–20mm out from the reference line you have just drawn. This will give a neat overhang when it is reinstalled and allows space for radiused corners. Take the trusty jigsaw and cut around the line, taking care to get a smooth and consistent curve on each of the radiuses.

Measure the lip on the edge of the appliances.

The small storage area is made in two pieces.

With the worktop cut to size and fitting correctly, remove it from the van and offer up the sink and cooker units. We decided to place the cooker on the right and the sink on the left, above the fridge, so that the cooker sits below the opening side window. With this arrangement, you can open the cooker lid and have the window open, allowing cooking smells outside to tempt your fellow campers, but keeping the hobs away from a direct breeze. If you are happy with the position of the appliances, make sure they are square to the front edges of the worktop and carefully mark around the edges.

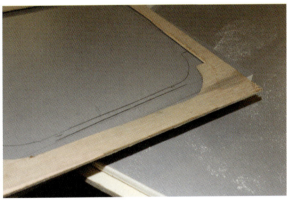

Sam Jeffery of VWorks has a template specifically for these appliances.

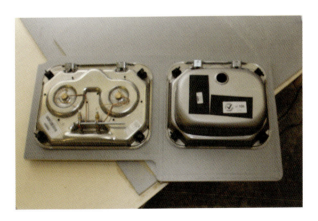

Marking the sink and cooker units.

A small flip-top cupboard was planned to the right of the cooker, which could double as a work surface when needed. This is a very simple arrangement. To build it, measure the size of the gap between the end of the main unit top and the vertical edge of the wardrobe, taking into account the space needed to fit an edging strip, and simply cut a square to match this space. Remove a 200mm section from the back; this will be the portion that remains fixed to the worktop, while the front section will lift up. The back left corner of this section will also need profiling to fit the window pillar.

Double-check the markings before cutting.

If you look at the edge of the cooker and sink units, you will see that there is a small return. This will overlap the worktop and prevent the unit simply falling through the hole. Measure the depth of the return (it will vary according to the precise appliance that you are using) and transfer the measurement to your worktop, marking a second line inside the one marking the outside edge of the unit. It is best to mark out the position of either the cooker or the sink first, then use this as a reference to align the second unit, as this will make it easier to spot if the two are misaligned.

Carefully jigsaw out the holes, avoiding making any chips in the veneer.

The appliances in place.

It is now time for the jigsaw again. Drill a pilot hole in the corner of each cut-out and work from there. Once the holes are cut, check that everything fits snugly. If it does, put the worktop back in the van, add the cooker and sink, and stand back and admire your handiwork.

CUPBOARD DOORS AND DRAWERS

You are not far now from having a completed interior; the last task is to build and fit the cupboard doors and drawer. With the drawers and doors fitted, you will have an interior that will provide all the functionality you will ever need.

The finished interior units, ready for camping.

Doors and drawers are very handy. Not only do they stop things falling out of your cupboards, they also make the interior of the van look nice and tidy. Exactly how you arrange your doors is down to personal taste, but it is worth taking some time to consider access. For example, are you likely to need to get into a cupboard when the bed is extended; if so, will the bed frame get in the way? In the case of our interior, the dimensions of the main cupboard under the cooker were dictated by the need to fit both the electrical control unit and the gas safe inside them. This in turn dictated the height of the internal shelf, which then had a knock-on effect on the location of the door latches.

Fitting

With the door height set, you will be able to measure the exact size of the front panel of the drawer, which will obviously dictate the size of the rest of the door. The drawer itself is simply an open-top box, while the runners were sourced from a local timber merchants. They run on ball bearings and the inner runner (the part that attaches to the drawer) is removable, making fitting easy. Drawers can be a little tricky to get right, but as long as you ensure that they are level and both runners are mounted at the same depth, you should not have too many problems.

making a box a home

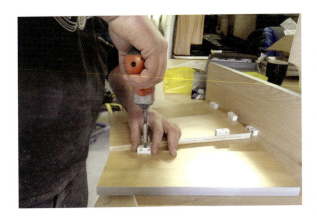

Assemble drawers in the same manner as the main cupboards.

Ensure sufficient clearance for the runners.

To construct the drawer, simply follow the same principles as for the rest of the interior units. However, it is important to take into account the clearance needed to allow the runners to fit between the drawer sides and the units. This will vary depending on the exact type used, but you want to ensure you are millimetre-perfect otherwise the action of the runner may be compromised.

Measure from the back of the cupboard to the back of the drawer front.

With the drawer built, place it in the aperture with the face flush with the front edges of the rest of the unit. Now measure from the back edge of the unit to the back face of the drawer facia. This will be the location of the front edge of the drawer runner. Again, accuracy here will result in a well-fitting drawer, although there is often a small degree of movement available thanks to elongated mounting holes in the runners.

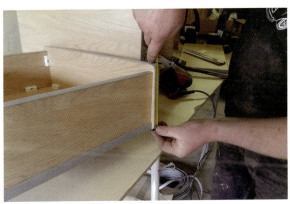

Find the centre point of the drawer sides.

It is best if the drawer runners are mounted dead centrally on the sides of the drawer. Measure the distance from the top edge of the drawer to the centre. This will be the distance to the centre of the runner from the lower edge of the facia panel on the cupboard unit; be sure to add a couple of millimetres for clearance. Transpose these measurements on to the inside of the cupboard unit; you should end up with marks showing the centre line of the drawer runner and its frontmost edge. Fix the runner into place using countersunk screws, ensuring that they do not stand proud and interfere with the runner operation.

Transfer the measurements to the unit.

making a box a home

Check the location of the runners.

Scribe the central line to the back of the drawer.

Use low-profile screws to prevent any snagging.

With the runners in place, the drawer should slide home.

Mark the centre point of the runner on the cupboard.

Double-check the distance to the centre of the runner from the bottom edge of the cupboard front and use this to mark the position of the other runner half on the drawer sides. Fix the runners in place and check that the drawer operates smoothly. You may find that some small adjustments are necessary, but, if you have measured accurately, it should be spot on.

Latches

There is a host of methods for securing doors and drawers shut, including catches, latches and even simple magnets. For our conversion, we chose pop-out catches, which are excellent. They sit flush with the panel when closed, but when they are pushed they pop out, releasing the door/drawer and providing a useful handle to pull on. They are a little more expensive than the friction-type latches found on most kitchen units, but they are stylish and reliable in operation. Additionally, fitting them is a doddle. They come in three parts: a latch mechanism, a knob and a collar. The collar slots through the front of the panel, providing a neat finish, while the mechanism screws to the back side.

Use a 25mm hole saw, being careful not to chip the veneer.

Mark the latch height.

The collar goes in first.

First, offer the latch up to the door, having ascertained what it will latch against. Measure the point from the centre of the latch to its upper and outer edges and use this to mark a centre point for drilling. Fortunately, these latches need a 20mm hole for the collar to fit through, which is a standard size. Drill a 20mm hole through the door, taking care not to damage the veneer. The collar can then be slotted into the hole; the ribbing will ensure a firm grip.

The latch mechanism goes in behind the collar.

Slot the latch through the hole from the inside and attach the knob. Set it to the closed position, ensure that it is straight and attach with a couple of screws. It is important to do this with the latch closed, otherwise you can end up with an offset between the knob and the collar, meaning the knob could get stuck in the hole if it catches the sides.

With the latch in the right place, all that is left to do is attach a keep for the latch to contact. These are simple right-angle fixings that screw to the woodwork. Fitting these can be a little tricky – you want them to be close enough to the latch that the door will not rattle, but not so close that the latch will not operate. The easiest way to get the keep in the right position is have someone hold the door shut and mark the location of the keep from the inside before screwing it in place.

Hold the door closed and fit the keeper.

6

beds and seating

The saying goes that you should spend your money on good shoes and a good bed, as you will spend a large proportion of your life in both. When it comes to your camper conversion, the same holds true – but, for shoes, substitute seats. You do not want to discover when you depart on the trip of a lifetime with your camper van that the bed is so uncomfortable that you cannot sleep a wink. Fortunately, VW has taken care of the seating situation, and the standard T5 seats are perfectly comfortable on long journeys – even those found in the most basic-specification transporters.

As for a bed, there are a number of routes you can take to nocturnal bliss, depending on your personal preference and of course on your budget. Do not think that you have to buy the most expensive bed system available in order to have a good night's sleep; I have spent many a happy night on an air bed in the back of a VW!

OPTIONS

When it comes to having a proper 'fitted' bed system, the cheapest option is to build your own 'rock and roll' set-up using a set of dedicated hinges that can be sourced from VW specialists such as Just Kampers. Combine these with some 18mm plywood or MDF and you can produce a perfectly functional bed for a minimal outlay. It should be noted that, because the original rock and roll beds were designed for rear-engined vans, which feature a raised rear floor, you will have to create a boxed section for use in a T5. You should also be aware that such a bed will have very little integrity in the event of a crash if it is used as passenger seating, as well as having no facility for seatbelts. If you do want to carry rear passengers, it is wise to stump up the cash for a more substantial steel-framed seat as a minimum.

The next step up from the classic rock and roll bed is a dedicated steel-framed, sliding bed. We chose this option for our van and it represents an excellent compromise between cost and quality. The seat used for this conversion was produced by Cheshire Motor Caravans (who also made the roof) and is a top-quality bit of kit. When in the upright position, it provides substantial seating accommodation for two adults and incorporates full three-point seatbelts. For sleeping duties, the seat can be folded completely flat with the simple pull of a handle. Its operation is very smooth thanks to ball-bearing sliders.

CMC offers two variants of the seat, a deluxe and standard, with the key difference being that one is crash certified and the other is not. The certified bed has been tested to withstand a set level of force applied in a variety of directions in order to simulate an accident. While there is no legal requirement to fit a certified bed in a van built for personal use, it is worth checking that your insurance company does not make such demands. Additionally, it goes without saying that, if you plan on carrying your family, conscience will demand that you fit a certified seat. However, this is not to say that non-certified seats are unsafe and the seat chosen for this conversion is the standard version. There is no doubt in my mind that it is eminently more structurally sound than the standard VW seating supplied in an older vintage van such as a T25 or Bay Window. The big caveat here is that, regardless of the seat type, if it is incorrectly fitted, all the crash testing in the world will not make it safe.

The bed frame from CMC.

A simple lever mechanism releases the bed frame.

beds and seating

The mechanism allows the bed to fold fully flat.

An 8.8 bolt rating should be a minimum requirement.

FITTING THE ROCK AND ROLL BED

The CMC bed is a substantial piece of kit and needs two people to lift it. The slide mechanism is operated by a lever located just below the seat base. To convert from a seat to a bed, you simply need to pull the lever sideways and tug the seat flat. Reversion back to a seat is equally straightforward.

Ensure the load bay is clear.

Regardless of how strong a bed is, it is useless if not correctly secured to the van. I have heard many tales of poorly fitted beds in vans, some from reputable conversion companies. These include seats that were simply screwed to ply flooring, or only held in place with a couple of small bolts through the vehicle floor. When looking at methods for mounting our seat, we referred to the stringent specifications relating to fitting seats in racing cars. From this, it was decided that four high-tensile M10 bolts would provide sufficient strength, combined with load-spreading plates under the floor. The bolts used were Allen-head stainless steel with a rating of 8.8. (Bolts come with a variety of ratings, which are stamped on the head. For those that may experience heavy loadings, 8.8 is considered a minimum rating.) Our bolts were left-over brake caliper mounting bolts from another project; if they were strong enough to cope with the loadings though a brake disc, they would be fine for our seat!

Load-spreading plates are necessary in order to prevent the bolts simply pulling through the relatively thin sheet metal of the van's floor. Our plates were constructed out of eighth-of-an-inch-thick steel plate about 2in (50mm) square, coated with hard-wearing paint to prevent them going rusty. It is also possible to use a single plate that stretches across the whole width of the van's floor.

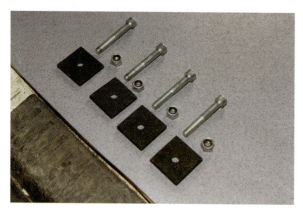

High-tensile mounting bolts and spreader washers.

The bed frame has a cut-out for the rear pillar.

beds and seating

Location of the bed in relation to the side door.

Measure from the bumper to the frame.

Check the bed folds out without hitting the sides.

Remove the spare wheel.

The position of the bed in the van will have an impact on the overall interior layout, particularly the location of the cupboard and kitchen units. The intention with our van was to maximize the space in the load bay, so the bed was located as far back and to the left as possible. Once you are happy with the location, check that the bed does not snag on any of the side panels as it is operated and ensure that the rear door will still shut. This bed had a cut-out in the rear corner that allowed it to be butted almost directly up to the door. The advantage of this is that, when the bed is in use, the tailgate will act as a headboard, to stop your pillows falling down under the frame.

The undertrays need to come out too (this is a messy job).

beds and seating

Measure from the rear edge of the bed to the edge of the rear bumper. This will be an important measurement for the next step. Next, move under the van to remove the spare wheel and protective undertrays, in order to access the van floor. This can be a bit of a tricky task, as these items are secured by a number of cross-head and hex-head screws and bolts, some of which are hard to find. With the trays out of the way, use the measurement from the seat base to the bumper to get an idea of where the bolt holes will come through the chassis. There are a number of box sections and reinforcements that can make life difficult; fortunately, the CMC bed has a good variety of mounting holes, so that they can be avoided.

With the bed positioned, mark the bolt holes.

Nut and spreader plate added.

Do not forget washers on the frame side.

Mark the position of the mounting holes, with a drill bit poked through the hole, then move the bed out of the way ready for drilling. Then drill each mounting hole in turn. Accuracy is important here – if the holes are even a few millimetres out of line it will be very difficult to locate the bolts. Remember the maxim: measure twice, cut once. With all of the holes drilled it is then simply a case of slotting the bolt home, fitting the spreader plates and tightening. In some areas, it was necessary to dress the van floor slightly to allow the plates to sit flat. Note that nyloc nuts were used, to prevent them working loose over time, as well as washers between the bolt heads and the seat frame.

Beware of strengthening ribs when drilling.

beds and seating

UPHOLSTERY

With the seat mounted in place, it is time to add some seat boards and upholstery. A good upholstery job can make or break the look of an interior. Poorly stitched seat covers and non-matching fabrics will not enhance the appearance of your van, so allow enough time to ensure that your upholstery is up to scratch. If you are handy with a sewing machine, or have access to someone who is, there is no reason why a set of basic seat covers cannot be made at home. However, for more complicated designs, it really does pay to get the professionals in. Sam Jeffery and wife Laura at VWorks are both experienced trimmers – whereas I struggle to thread a needle – so responsibility for this part of the work on our van was left to them.

Checking the fit in the van.

Coat the bed boards with contact adhesive.

Attach the bed boards to the pre-cut foam.

The completed foam and boards.

The seat used in this conversion features an open framework that needs boards making to provide support for the cushions. These are constructed out of 12mm ply, cut to the size of each portion of the seat. Measure the dimensions of each face of the seat and add a few millimetres each side to ensure that the seat frame is not visible once the cushions are fitted. Unlike in some older vans with rock and roll beds, the cushions will be permanently attached to the seat bases once finished.

beds and seating

Foam forms the bulk of the seat and is available in a variety of different thicknesses and densities. For this build, we chose a 3-inch (75mm) thick, medium-density foam. Cutting foam can be a bit tricky, but luckily most foam suppliers can provide a cutting service (customcutfoams.co.uk is a good bet). Simply provide them with the measurements for the base boards and you receive perfectly square pieces with nice straight edges. The foam then needs to be glued to the bed boards, using the same contact adhesive as for the carpet lining.

VW Inca fabric sourced online.

Grey vinyl was a bargain at £10 per metre.

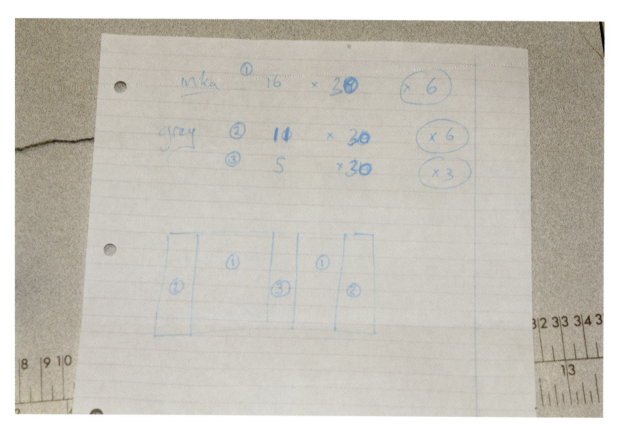

Make a plan of the cushions to avoid confusion.

Material choice is a subjective one but, unless you are also re-trimming the front seats, it makes sense to make the rear seats match. VW pattern fabric is available from a number of retailers so you should be able to find some to match existing upholstery. The 'Inca' fabric used for these seats was sourced from an eBay seller for around £25 per metre, and came on a 1,700mm-wide roll; trimming a standard-sized bed requires at least 2m of fabric. Its foam 'scrim' backing provides it with more structure than a simpler fabric. To provide a bit of contrast, we also purchased some plain grey vinyl.

Stitch along the back of the fabric first.

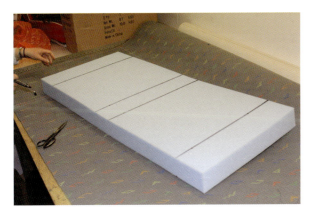

The fabric pattern marked on the foam.

Leave about 10mm excess fabric at the seams.

Marking out the fabric sections.

The fabric doubled over ready for stitching.

Before cutting any fabric, measure the size of each bed section and calculate the area of material needed for each one, allowing for the height and about 100mm to return under the bed board. Use the seat foam as a guide for marking out the individual pieces of fabric. In our van, each seat centre was divided by a 100mm strip of grey vinyl, which in turn dictated the width of the fabric sections. Once you are happy with the measurements, it is time to start marking the fabric. This is done using a white pencil or chalk, ensuring that you leave a 10mm overlap on each section; this is the part that will be stitched.

Stitch along the front of the fabric.

beds and seating

A heavy-duty industrial sewing machine will make light work of most fabrics, but a regular domestic machine will suffice for thin fabric and vinyl. Place the corresponding sections of fabric together and stitch them along the backside first. A good tip is to draw a line where the stitches will go, to make it easier to sew a straight edge. Once the initial seams have been sewn, each panel is then front stitched. This involves folding each seam back on itself and then running a stitch along the outside of the fabric. If this is not done, the result would be unsightly sags along the edges of each cushion. Depending on how creative you feel, this stitch can be made with a contrasting thread.

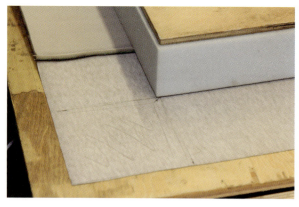

Mark out the corner cuts.

Once all of the panels have been stitched together they need to be oriented on the seat bases. To achieve this, find the central points on both the long and the short sides of the fabric and the seat base, then place the seat base upside down on the backside of the covers. If the marks are correctly lined up you can confirm the corner locations and start to mark the areas to remove at each corner of the fabric. Again, remember to leave a 10mm edge to be stitched on each flap. With all of the excess material removed, stitch each corner together so that the fabric forms an open-topped box.

The fabric sections all joined together.

Find the centre of the fabric and cushion.

With the corners stitched, the seat should slot into the fabric 'box'.

Start stapling at the corners, holding the fabric tight.

beds and seating

Ensure the staples are in a straight line.

If you have cut and stitched the material correctly, it should fit snugly over the foam and bed board. All that remains is to fit it securely in place. This is done with staples, using a regular manual staple gun or an air or electric-powered gun (which is much easier). Starting at the corners will help you to stretch out any ruffles along the way. You want to pull the fabric tight over the foam, but not so tight that the seams are over-stretched; you also need to be careful not to pull the fabric off-centre. To ensure that the fabric cannot come astray, the staples should be approximately 25mm apart.

The finished cushions ready for fitting.

Screw the cushions in place from underneath.

FITTING THE SEAT PANELS

With all of the seat panels covered, it is time to fit them into the van. It pays to take some time doing this as the alignment of the cushions relative to each other and to the van will have an impact on the whole aesthetic. The bases are attached using screws that run through the seat frame. Standard wood screws do the job perfectly – in this case 35mm screws were used. If the screws are too long they will protrude into the foam, leading to potential posterior piercing. Drill six evenly spaced holes along the back and front rails of each seat section.

Place the boards on to the bed with it laid flat, leaving a small gap between each one. On some beds the cushions can be butted directly up to each other, but with this hinge design this will cause the fabric to ruck up when the bed returns to being a seat. It can take a bit of trial and error to get the cushion position just right, so initially only attach each board with a couple of screws until you are certain of the final position.

Once the boards are fully attached you should have a comfortable bed and functioning rear seat. If the slight gaps between each cushion bother you, the best solution is to purchase a 1-inch (25mm) thick 'memory foam' mattress topper. This will provide a smooth sleeping surface and can be easily rolled up and stored when not in use.

SWIVEL FRONT SEAT

Next to adding a pop-top, one of the most effective things you can do to increase the available space in your van is to fit rotating front seats, also known as 'captain's chairs'. Some vans, including those that have a single front passenger seat, come with these as standard. If you are not lucky enough to have such a specification of van, it is possible to retro-fit one.

As with the majority of conversion jobs, the approach you take will depend on the budget available. The easiest option is to source a standard VW captain's chair, but these are not cheap – they retail for anything up to £600 on the second-hand market. It should also be noted that, if you replace a double front passenger seat, as found in most panel vans, with a single, the rubber cab mat will also need to be swapped for one with different cut-outs.

A second option, if you already have a single passenger seat or simply want to be able to move the driver's seat, is to use an aftermarket swivel base. This bolts on to the standard seat base and allows it to be turned. If you convert the driver's seat in this way, though, it will normally be necessary to relocate the handbrake lever to allow the seat to rotate. If this is your chosen route, most suppliers of rotating bases will also be able to provide a relocation kit for this purpose.

beds and seating

The third solution, and the approach chosen for our van, has been available only fairly recently. It consists of a large swivel base mechanism that allows for a double passenger seat to be rotated to face the rear of the van. For this particular conversion, it seemed the most sensible option, both from a cost perspective and in terms of space utilization. With the seat rotated, it provides comfortable accommodation for at least five adults and, at a push, six. While the operation of such a set-up is not quite as slick as a VW factory swivel, it is by no means complicated and, at a cost of around £200 for such a conversion base, it is the most cost-effective option for a factory-fitted double seat. Fitting is also a refreshingly simple task.

The seat is locked in place with four clamp bolts.

The swivel base comes as a single piece and its operation is quite simple. It consists of a top and bottom plate, separated by nylon section that facilitates smooth movement between the plates. The lower plate is bolted to the floor of the van, using the existing fixing studs, while the upper plate features studs that slot into the holes in the seat frame. The two plates are secured together by four threaded fixings, locking the seat facing either forwards or backwards.

Remove the passenger seat.

To kick things off, remove the front passenger seat by undoing the eight bolts that secure it in place. It is also necessary to unclip the wiring connections that are housed in the base. The seat is heavy, so it is a good idea to enlist some help to pull it out. With the seat removed, you can access a small flap in the floor mat; under there you should find a small recess into which you can push the wiring.

Studs may need to be trimmed.

The swivel seat base.

Fit the base over the studs.

beds and seating

The base needs to be rotated to access fixing bolts.

Loosen the adjusters.

Refit the seat – do not forget any nuts.

Before the base can be fitted in place, a few millimetres need to be trimmed off the mounting studs. If this is not done, the studs sit too high and catch on the upper plate, preventing proper rotation. With the studs trimmed, place the base on to the studs and reaffix the securing nuts. It is necessary to slide the upper plate around in order to access all of the fixings and a flexible extension bit can help with access. The seat can then be placed on to the mounting studs – again, a helping hand is useful when it comes to lining up the studs with the holes. Make sure that all the nuts are done up tightly; you do not want the seat working loose.

The seat needs to be shunted to rotate.

beds and seating

Alternatively, the seat may be positioned parallel to the door opening.

Seating capacity in the rear is now doubled.

To rotate the base, first ensure that all the fixing bolts are loosened off, then slide the seat around towards the door opening – some shifting back and forth may be needed to achieve this. Once the seat is fully rotated, relocate the fixing bolts and secure it in place. Lo and behold, you now have seating for the whole family in the back.

ROOF BED

Having a pop-top roof is an exceptionally good way of increasing the space available in your camper and, with a little extra work, it can be made even more effective, providing additional living and sleeping space. This is achieved by fitting a roof bed; when you are using the van during the day, it can be raised, then it can be lowered at night to provide accommodation for two (medium-sized) people.

Compared to the effort of adding the pop-top in the first place, installing a roof bed is a very simple task. There are a number of different routes to achieving this. The first and simplest, but most expensive, option is to purchase one from a company such as Reimo, or directly from your roof supplier. Costs vary, but it should be between £300 and £500. There are also a number of suppliers selling kits that comprise all the necessary components, such as hinges and struts, leaving you to add the bed boards. We opted for the third option for our van: building one completely from scratch. It takes a bit more effort but it is by far the most cost-effective, with the total expense for this bed being in the region of £75.

The materials needed are very basic: a single 8 × 4ft sheet of 18mm plywood, two lengths of piano hinge, a pair of stepped hinges, and some carpet. For the construction, the same basic tools needed for the interior units will suffice, and a basic circular table saw will be a useful addition.

Measure the size of the roof area.

beds and seating

Measure the width of the roof area too.

Check the height of the vertical section of bed.

To begin with, elevate the pop-top and measure the size of the aperture. The side reinforcing rails have a step that serves to locate a bed board. Measure the distance between the steps and allow 10mm each side for clearance. (The dimensions shown in the plan are specific to our particular van; double-check that your conversion matches them.)

The bed is constructed in four sections, one of which attaches to the roof side rails, to allow for the mounting of the hinges. This is necessary as it is not possible to mount the hinges directly to the roof due to its curvature. When cutting the respective sections, a long section of metal angle or similar is useful for ensuring a straight line. Simply clamp it to the piece of wood you wish to cut and use it as a guide for the circular saw. Once the rearmost section of bed is cut and checked for fit, it is a good idea to reinforce the edge using a piece of aluminium c-channel. This will provide some much-needed stiffness for the hinge mountings. This section is then attached to the roof side rails using four self-tapping screws.

Once this section is fixed in place, measure the distance from the edge of the reinforcement to the top of the roof; this will be the length of the second roof section, which will hinge upwards in order to maximize head room.

Mark up a sheet of 18mm ply.

Fix the rear hinges.

Aluminium reinforcement for the hinge section.

beds and seating

Offset hinges can be bought from most builders' merchants.

The correct non-countersunk screws.

Fix the piano hinge with non-countersunk screws.

Note that the screws do not distort the hinge.

Offset hinges are needed to attach the first movable section of the bed. These are affixed to the reinforcement bar and allow the section to hinge until it is vertical. The hinges can be found in most decent timber merchants or from companies such as Screwfix. Once the hinged section is affixed in place, measure and cut the remaining two pieces – the small front section is necessary to aid access to the bed space when in use. These sections are then attached using the piano hinge, ensuring that the hinge is correctly oriented to allow for the bed to hinge upwards.

In order to check the fit and location of each section, it is easiest to assemble the bed in place before removing it for finishing. With the bed laid out on the work bench it is easier to check that each of the sections aligns properly, prior to screwing all of the piano hinges permanently in place. A word of warning: a piano hinge can be very susceptible to flexing if it is not attached along its entire length, and this can permanently twist and damage it. As a result of this weakness you will need to be very careful to support the bed when it is being moved to and from the van. It is also important to use the correct type of screw to secure the hinge. A dome-headed screw with a flat underside is needed; if a countersunk screw is used, it can easily deform the delicate hinge, making it stiff to operate.

The main bed assembled.

beds and seating

The start of the carpet covering.

This return allows the front section to fold upwards.

Spray liberally with contact adhesive.

With all of the hinges properly secured, the bed can be trimmed to match the rest of the van's lining. If this is done properly, it is possible to create a seamless sheet of carpet on the underside of the bed – the part that will be visible from inside the van. Start by spraying both the carpet and the bed boards with contact adhesive on the lower side (the side that forms the roof of the van). When trimming, either carpet or upholstery, a hooked blade on a Stanley knife is the ideal tool to make fast, accurate cuts. When it comes to trimming carpet, ensure that you always have a sharp blade fitted. If it is at all dull it will snag and create a jagged cut. In order to allow the front section of the bed to hinge upwards, it is necessary to leave a roll of loose carpet at the joint. It is a little tricky to ensure that an even roll is created, but with care it is possible. The most important consideration is to ensure that no glue gets on the vertical edge of the joint as the carpet will bunch up on it.

A carpet-cutting blade.

A heavier grade of carpet was used on the bed top, to give better resistance to wear.

beds and seating

The finished item, ready for use.

The sleeping area will easily accommodate two adults.

A load-bay securing eyelet reused to support the bed in its elevated position.

The choice of finish on the top of the bed is down to personal choice. It would be perfectly feasible to incorporate a couple of inches of mattress foam into each section and trim with fabric. However, for our bed we chose to use a carpet lining. The carpet is slightly tougher and less flexible than that used to cover the inside of the van, which will make it less susceptible to wear from heavy use.

Once the bed is refitted, the last task is to create a method of securing it in the 'up' position when not in use. Many kits use gas struts and support rods, which undoubtedly make for a very easy lifting process. However, the bed is not at all heavy, and struts and rods can introduce unnecessary complications. Instead, a simple system of clips and straps was devised for our project, utilizing the now redundant load-bay mounting eyelets. These were mounted to the pop-top, using the same sealed washers as were used to attach the pop-top tie-downs. One eyelet was attached on either side of the roof and a pair of tie-down eyelets to the bed. Securing the roof is then simply a matter of clipping up the straps using a small spring-gate karabiner.

The roof bed effectively doubles the sleeping capacity of the van and is a very worthwhile addition. Obviously you can improve upon this design if you wish. For example, it would be an easy task to run wiring along the bed boards under the carpet in order to provide a reading light or similar.

beds and seating

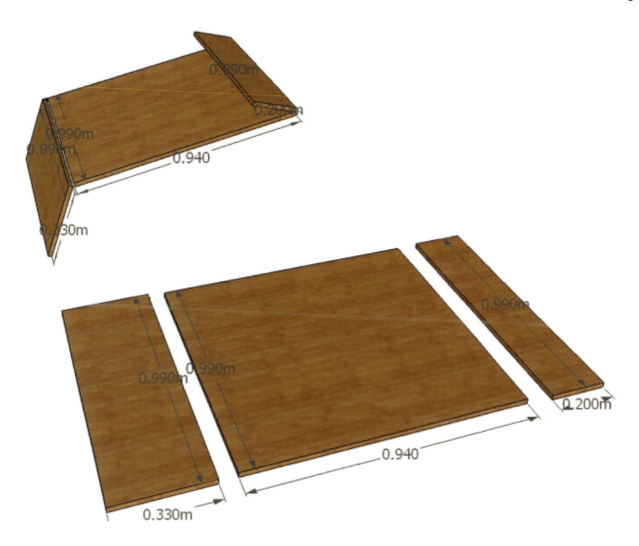

Dimensions of roof-bed sections; you will need to double-check your own installation.

7

gas and water

There is no hard and fast rule as to what gas-fired gear and water supply you need in order to be comfortable in a camper van. Before being converted, our van provided perfectly comfortable accommodation for a two-week trip around the Alps and a trip to the Le Mans 24-hr race, with nothing more than a 12V cool box and a cartridge-type camping stove. However, a properly fitted set of interior appliances does make for a more civilized environment and thus it was decided that this van would get everything needed to make it a self-contained home.

The intention with our van was to keep things simple, yet provide the capacity to add more kit at a later date. The list of requirements was as follows:

- a 240V hook-up for longer-term stays on campsites;
- a split charging system;
- centralized power control;
- flexible interior lighting;
- a fridge;
- sufficient power outlets to charge a couple of phones and a laptop simultaneously;
- a two-burner hob;
- a sink with running water.

This is quite a lot of equipment to cram into the confines of a T5 and at first glance the task of ensuring it is all installed correctly can be a little daunting. However, as with all of the tasks on the van, it is (relatively) simple, provided you take things slowly and methodically.

For advice on installing a power-management system and electrical devices, *see* Chapter 8.

Stand-alone Smev sink.

A circular variant of sink is available, if preferred.

A triple-burner Smev hob.

88

gas and water

A combination sink/hob unit from Smev.

> ### SAFETY FIRST
>
> All work relating to gas and electricity supplies can cause dangerous problems if it is not carried out correctly. At best, the outcome could be damage to your van; at worst it could be fatal to you. If you are at all unsure about your capability to safely undertake any of the tasks detailed, or about any points at all, you must consult or employ a professional. Even if you are completely happy that you know what you are doing, it is still advisable to get your gas and electric systems checked over by a certified gas fitter or electrician to ensure that you have not missed anything.
>
> The set-up used in our van was designed to be very simple to install and connect, in the hope of minimizing the chance of a DIY installer making mistakes. Even so, I strongly recommend that you get any work double-checked, for safety's sake.

FRIDGES AND COOL BOXES

Keeping fresh food (or beer) cool is a vital requirement if you are planning on using your van for more than a couple of days at a time. There are a number of ways to incorporate a fridge or cool box into the vehicle, each with its own benefits and disadvantages.

The first option is a compressor-type fridge. This is the same type of fridge that you use in your home. On the upside, a fridge of this type is generally much cheaper than an absorption-type fridge (*see* below). Compressor fridges work by pumping a refrigerant liquid around a system of tubes to draw heat out from the inside of the fridge and transfer it to the outside air. A sensor inside the fridge monitors the temperature and turns on the compressor when it rises above a certain point. The compressor pumps the refrigerant through a series of metal heat-exchanger coils on the back of the fridge.

The big benefit of a compressor fridge is that it runs solely on electrical power – 12V and 12/240V units are available – so no venting is required, as is the case with '3-way' fridges that also run on gas. The disadvantage is that, if you do not have access to a mains hook-up, the fridge will be constantly drawing from your leisure battery when the engine is not running. However, the current draw of the latest generation of compressor fridges is not huge, in the region of 0.4 A/h (compared to some 3-way fridges, which can draw up to 9A/h when running solely on electricity). Thanks to this low current draw, it is also feasible to run a compressor fridge on power provided by a solar panel, reducing the strain on the leisure battery.

The second option is an absorption-type fridge, also referred to as a 3-way fridge. These are generally found in large motorhomes and caravans, but installation in a small van, such as a T4 or T5, can be a bit trickier. A 3-way fridge can run on 12V, 240V or gas power and, like a compressor fridge, uses a refrigerant with a very low boiling point. When it evaporates, the refrigerant removes heat from the unit. However, rather than using a pump and heat exchanger, an absorption fridge uses a heat source – the gas flame – for power.

The advantage of an absorption fridge it that it does not have to rely on electricity, so running it will not drain your leisure battery if mains power is not available. However, the disadvantage is that such a fridge requires a gas vent to be cut in the side of the van to allow the fumes from the combustion process to escape.

The final solution is simply to use a 12V cool box that can be removed from the van. This is the cheapest option, but a cool box is not as efficient as either an absorption or a compressor fridge.

The main suppliers of fridges intended for motorhome use are Waeco and Dometic, both of whom supply units ranging from cool boxes to large-capacity 3-way fridges. For this project we opted to use a Waeco MDC 50 12V compressor fridge. The main reason for this choice was simplicity of wiring and fitting, with no internal vents required. The compact unit provides plenty of internal space – more than enough to store milk and other fresh goods – and even incorporates a small freezer unit. It has a power input of 45W and, according to Waeco's specifications, only consumes an average of 0.8A/h.

gas and water

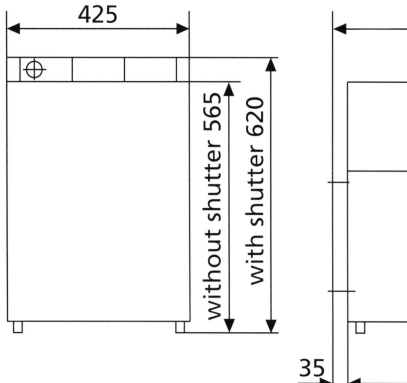

Dimensions of the Waeco MDC50 fridge.

The Waeco MDC50 12V fridge.

COOKING APPLIANCES

It is a great joy in a camper van to be able to wake up in the morning and cook a tasty bacon sandwich and make a cup of tea. To achieve this, you will need some form of cooker. This can be as simple as a portable camping gas stove, but a far superior solution is to have a fitted cooker.

There is a bewildering array of different hobs and even combined hob/grill units available on the market. For our van, we simply wanted a decent twin-burner hob, which would allow for cooking with two pans, and provide enough capacity to create amazing culinary camping delights. We chose a Smev 8000 series, which features two burners and is also available with a Piezo ignition system, to save messing about with matches. A number of other varieties are available, but this unit is one that provides a good compromise between cost and quality.

The most significant consideration with any gas system is safety. Any installation needs to be safe, to prevent carbon-monoxide poisoning, or the system blowing up or catching fire.

Gas Types

All gas used for camping appliances is known as LPG (Liquid Petroleum Gas), but it is generally available in two types: butane and propane. There is little difference between the two gases, except that propane works better at lower temperatures than butane. This is worth considering if you are thinking of winter skiing tours in your van, although, as the

gas and water

cylinder will be inside the vehicle, it should not be too much of a worry.

It is also worth noting that, until September 2003, caravans and motorhomes used a different regulator depending on which gas was being used to provide the appropriate operating pressures – 28mbar (millibar) for butane and 37mbar for propane. Some units from European countries used different pressures, of up to 50mbar. Since September 2003 a European standard (EN 1949) has made the supply pressure the same for both gases throughout the EU, at 30mbar. While pre-2003 units still require different regulators depending on the gas used, all current UK-built caravans run at 30mbar, and this figure should be marked in the gas locker near to the regulator. Although most people will be using brand-new kit, this information should be considered if you are working with second-hand parts.

The final question relating to gas choice is what type and size of bottle to use. The easy answer here is to use a Camping Gaz 907 type bottle. There are a bewildering array of other sizes and types of bottle on the market, such as those from Calor, but, for 99 per cent of T4 and T5 conversions, this particular bottle is most suitable, for a number of reasons:

♦ It is compact, measuring only 10in (250mm) high with a diameter of just over 8in (203mm). This means that it only requires a small gas safe, which can be easily incorporated into an interior design.
♦ It can hold up to 2.75kg of butane, which will run a double-burner stove for approximately 8 hours. This should be more than sufficient for most trips.
♦ Most importantly, it is easy to source abroad. It is almost impossible to find Calor Gas in Europe, but you should find Camping Gaz refills everywhere.

The regulator for the 907.

Installation

The cooker installation for our van was about as basic as it could be. The components of the system consisted of the following:

♦ Smev twin-burner hob;
♦ 1m of flexible gas pipe;
♦ a Camping Gaz 907 bottle and regulator; and
♦ a coupling from the stove to the gas pipe.

The gas cylinder is located in a steel gas safe in the cupboard underneath the cooker, so the pipe run is less than 1m. This means that it is perfectly acceptable to use a flexible hose. If the pipe run is over 1.5m, solid copper tubing should be used, for safety reasons.

Thermocouple gas cut-offs.

Camping Gaz 907 bottle is the best bet for size and ease of finding refills.

The component of the pipe union.

gas and water

Fit the collar first.

Attaching the fitting to the cooker is the hardest part of the installation. Anything to do with gas requires care, but this work needs particular attention. Each burner has a cut-off valve, which features a thermocouple switch that cuts the gas supply if no flame is detected. This prevents any leaking if the gas is left on unlit or blows out. To attach the flexible hose, a coupler needs to be added. These can be purchased from most camping shops and consist of a couple, a nut and a copper olive. These are slid over the pipe and, as the nut is tightened, the olive crushes, sealing the joint with the pipe. Be careful not to over-tighten the nut and do not use any jointing compound or PTFE, as this can actually cause a leak.

WATER SUPPLIES

After the collar, fit the olive and then the end piece.

The tap unit to fit the sink.

Slide the components together.

An in-tank pump will supply water to the tap.

Be sure not to over-tighten the fitting.

Water hose was sourced from a local caravan supply centre.

SAFETY

Certification and good practice

Interestingly, there are currently no regulations dictating gas-system standards for home-built campers. Anyone can undertake their own gas installation, provided the vehicle is not going to be rented out. However, some insurance companies do insist that any gas installations are certified, so check if you are unsure.

Even if your van does not require a certificate, it is worth looking at the certification and the areas that it covers as it provides a sound guide for good practice. The Gas Safe certificate is provided by the Gas Safe register in the UK, which replaced CORGI, the body with which most people will be familiar. It can be issued only by a certified gas fitter, with the specific qualifications to deal with gas installations in motorhomes. To receive a Gas Safe certificate, the installation must comply with British Standard BS EN 1949. Unfortunately, this is copyrighted, but a copy can be obtained from BSIGroup.com for a fee.

To ensure you have the safest gas installation possible, regardless of whether you plan on getting it certified or not, there are a number of key considerations:

- Ensure that dedicated LPG gas hose is used. For applications where the pipe run between the bottle and cooker is more than 1.5m, it is highly recommended that solid copper pipe is used. Pipe should be secured to prevent excessive movement that could cause it to degrade. Flexible pipes should be checked for condition at least annually and replaced regardless of condition every five years.
- Ensure that your gas bottle has the correct regulator.
- The gas bottle should be kept in a sealed box with at least half-hour fire rating, often referred to as a 'gas safe'. The box can be either steel or glass fibre, provided it is fire proof.
- Ensure that there is at least one drop vent for the gas bottle. LPG is heavier than air and thus sinks. A drop vent is a vent in the floor of the van, next to the gas bottle, that allows any leaking gas to vent to the outside atmosphere.
- Make sure that the hob you use has a built-in gas cut-off. This consists of a thermostatically controlled valve on the gas supply to each burner. If no flame is detected, the gas supply remains cut off, preventing an inadvertent leak.

Government guidance

Although there are no requirements for certification of gas appliances (which includes gas fridges) in private-use camper vans, the UK Government does require that any installations comply with the Road Vehicles (Construction and Use) Regulations, 1986. Specifically, this means regulations 95 and 96, which state the following (Regulation 95):

1. No person shall use, or cause or permit to be used, in or on a vehicle on a road any gas-fired appliance unless the whole of such appliance and the gas system attached thereto is in an efficient and safe condition.
2. No person shall use, or cause or permit to be used, in any gas-fired appliance in or on a vehicle on a road any fuel except liquefied petroleum gas as defined in regulation 94 (4).
3. No person shall use, or cause or permit to be used, in or on a vehicle on a road any gas-fired appliance unless the vehicle is so ventilated that (a) an ample supply of air is available for the operation of the appliance; (b) the use of the appliance does not adversely affect the health or comfort of any person using the vehicle; and (c) any unburnt gas is safely disposed of to the outside of the vehicle.
4. No person shall use, or cause or permit to be used, on a road a vehicle in or on which there is (a) one gas-fired appliance unless the gas supply for such appliance is shut off at the point where it leaves the container or containers at all times when the appliance is not in use; (b) more than one gas-fired appliance each of which has the same supply of gas unless the gas supply for such appliances is shut off at the point where it leaves the container or containers at all times when none of such appliance is in use; or (c) more than one gas-fired appliance each of which does not have the same supply of gas unless each gas supply for such appliances is shut off at the point where it leaves the container or containers at all times when none of such appliances which it supplies is in use.

Regulation 96 deals with gas heating and refrigeration. The most important part is paragraph 5, which states that 'No person shall use, or cause or permit to be used, in a vehicle to which this regulation applies which is in motion on a road any gas-fired appliance unless it is fitted with a valve which stops the supply of gas to the appliance if the appliance fails to perform its function and causes gas to be emitted.'

gas and water

Having running water in your van is a nice luxury, and is very simple to achieve, with a tap, some hose and a pipe. The tap we chose is designed specifically to fold away when the sink is closed and features an in-built micro-switch to control the flow of water. This switch is connected to a submersible pump that sits within the water container, which in turn is fixed to a 12V supply. The pump is fed electricity via a cable that runs through the tap switch, with the power supplied by the onboard power-management system. All of this equipment, including the pipe, was obtained from a local caravan supply centre, where staff were able to advise that the respective parts would be compatible with each other. Obviously it is important to ensure that the pipe work is long enough to reach the water container.

A 25mm hole saw suited the size of the tap thread.

The sink has a recess to accept the tap.

Carefully drill the hole. You may want to mask the surrounding area.

Find and mark the central point.

The SMEV sink did not come with a hole for a tap pre-cut, so it was necessary to create one. Measure the distance from the back edge of the sink to the start of the basin, then mark a centre point for the tap hole that is equidistant from these two points. Put some masking tape around the area to prevent damage in case the cutter slips, and use a sharp 25mm hole cutter to create the hole. The cutter will leave a rough edge, which will need to be filed smooth.

De-burr the edges of the hole.

gas and water

The tap is secured by a plastic lock nut.

The location of the water container below the wardrobe.

All that remains is to connect the wiring.

It is possible to buy custom-made water containers that can be fitted either internally or externally to the van. CAK Tanks is one company that produces an internal tank specifically for the T5, which is moulded to the shape of the inner wheel arch. However, such tanks are expensive and so for this conversion we opted for a basic 25-litre plastic jerry can. It is not the most sophisticated solution but it does have its benefits. Beyond being cheap (about £20), it can also be carried easily from the van to a convenient water point, negating the need to drive the van to a tap and hose. Conveniently (and this was more by happy circumstance than by design) it also fitted neatly into the space between the inner wheel arch and the bed, tucked away at the bottom of the cupboard.

The tap is secured in place using a plastic nut, with a gasket to create a seal between the two. Do not do the nut up too tightly, as it is easy to strip the thread. With the sink fitted into the interior units, connect one end of the wiring to the positive connection on the pump. The other wire is then connected to the power-management system; in the case of the unit used in our van there is a dedicated 'tap' connection.

The container cap was adapted to accept the water hose and cable.

A 25-litre jerry can.

gas and water

Slide the hose and cable through the cap.

The pump is then attached.

The water tank came with a standard plastic screw-on cap, which needed some modification in order to fit an internal pump. This was achieved using a stepped drill bit to drill a hole large enough to accept a rubber grommet. A smaller hole was then drilled to accommodate the power cable for the pump. The hose and cable were then threaded through these holes, with the rubber grommet preventing any leakage from the water sloshing around while the van is moving.

When the tank needs to be filled, the cap can be unscrewed and removed, pump and all, and the tank removed from the vehicle. A spare cap was purchased to allow the tank to be completely sealed off if necessary.

It is possible to fit a waste-water tank under the can to catch the run-off from the sink, but we decided simply to route the waste pipe (also purchased from a local caravan store) out through the floor of the van.

8

electricity

Remember! If you are not confident in your ability to undertake any of this potentially dangerous work, you should employ a professional. If you do decide to do the work yourself, it is recommended that you get it checked over by a certified electrician.

THE BASICS

An Electrical Circuit

Electricity is a fundamental part of many of the functions in your camper van. It is therefore a good idea to have some understanding of basic electrical theory before getting stuck in to the wiring of your conversion. This is not intended to be a comprehensive school lesson but it should help you understand why the various parts of the wiring are as they are. Not only will this be useful during your build, it will also make life a lot easier if you have problems further down the line or want to add additional functionality to the basic systems included in this build.

In its most simple form, an electrical circuit consists of three fundamental parts:

1. A power source to drive electrical current around the circuit (a battery);
2. A conductor to carry the current around the circuit (some cable);
3. A load that has resistance (a bulb, a heating element, a motor and so on) and converts the electrical energy into another form (light, heat, kinetic and so on).

The conductor is used to connect the positive side of the power source to the load, which is then connected back to the negative side of the power source to complete the circuit. A current will then flow through the load, converting stored energy in the battery to another form.

Most circuits will also often include other components such as switches, resistors, diodes, capacitors, fuses, relays and so on, but these three fundamental parts will always be present in every electrical circuit.

Terms Used

There are a number of terms that need to be understood when working with electrical circuits:

- Volts (V): measure of electrical potential difference between two points in a circuit. In most modern passenger cars and light commercial vehicles this is 12V, however larger commercial vehicles and agricultural equipment may use 24V.
- Amperes (A): measure of the amount of electric charge flowing past a point in a circuit in a given amount of time (commonly abbreviated to 'amps')
- Ohms (R): measure of electrical resistance to the flow of charge in a circuit.
- Watts (P): power, which is a measure of the rate at which an electrical circuit converts electrical energy into another form

The easiest way to understand these terms and the relationship they have to each other is to compare an electrical circuit with a plumbing system. In this analogy, volts are equivalent to the water pressure in the plumbing system, amps represent the flow rate of water through the pipes while the ohms value relates to the size of the pipe.

A watt is a universal measurement of energy conversion (or 'work done'), so it applies equally to water systems as it does to electrical systems. For example, a garden sprinkler will have 'power' due to the rate at which it converts the energy in the water into rotation, just as a light bulb will have a power as it converts electrical energy into light and heat.

This analogy can be continued when thinking about changing these values:

- If you increase water pressure then more water will flow in a given amount of time.
- Similarly, if you increase voltage then more current will flow in a given amount of time.
- If you reduce the size of the pipes then less water will flow in a given amount of time. Similarly, if you increase resistance then less current will flow in a given amount of time.

Current and Current Flow

The type of current usually found in vehicle electrical systems is direct current (DC), where the flow of charge is in one direction and the voltage level is constant. However, in a camper van, you will also find alternating current (AC) in the 240V circuits, where the flow of charge is in both directions and the voltage changes with time. Your van's alternator also produces AC current but it is converted to DC before it is input to the battery.

The conventional way of thinking about current flow in a circuit is that it flows from the positive terminal of the battery to the negative terminal (or ground). Current flow is the movement of free electrons within the conductor and since electrons are negatively charged they actually migrate towards the +ve terminal of the battery when subject to a voltage difference, so current flow is from –ve to +ve. This

electricity

concept is fairly counter-intuitive for most people and so the convention of current flow being from +ve to –ve has stuck. Actually, it makes little practical difference.

Ground

In order for an electrical circuit to be complete, the positive terminal of the battery must be connected through the loads and back to the negative terminal, otherwise current cannot flow. In most vehicles the negative terminal of the battery is normally connected to the metal chassis, which is a good conductor and effectively makes the entire chassis (and body of the vehicle, if metallic) a common ground point. The chassis can then be thought of as a large extension of the negative battery terminal and proves very convenient for grounding different parts of the electrical system, as there is normally a suitable chassis (or body) location close by to complete the circuit. This is only possible because of the use of rubber tyres, which virtually insulate the vehicle from earth, preventing current leakage. In fact, tyres do conduct slightly due to the carbon content in the rubber, which helps remove static build-up, but the resistance is relatively high and so the effect on the electrical system is very small.

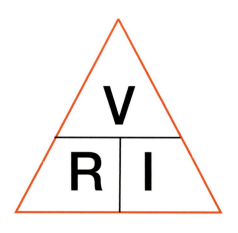

$$\frac{V}{R} = I \qquad \frac{V}{I} = R$$

$$R \times I = V$$

$$\frac{P}{V} = I \qquad \frac{P}{I} = V$$

$$V \times I = P$$

Basic electrical formulae. P = power, V = volts, I = current (in amps), R = resistance (in ohms).

Volts, Amps, Ohms and Watts

The relationship between the various values is described in two very simple equations, allowing you to calculate any unknown value as long as you know the two others:

Ohm's Law, which states the relationship of voltage to current and resistance: Volts (V) = Current (I) × Resistance (R).

Watt's Law, which states the relationship of power to voltage, current and resistance: Power (P) = Volts (V) × Current (I).

For a given power requirement, a higher voltage will require fewer amps and vice versa. This is the reason that circuits operating at 12V DC can produce much higher currents than would be experienced in household AC circuits that operate at 240V AC. For example, you will rarely find a 20-amp fuse in a household wiring system, even on an electric cooker, but in a car, this will be the minimum for a circuit such as a headlight.

There is a third equation – Current (I) = Power/Voltage – which is used for calculating the current drawn by a load, whether it is a light bulb or a toaster. It is very useful because it will allow you to pick the right-sized cable for various applications. (Cables have different current ratings.) For example, the 12V sockets used in this conversion have a power rating of 120W. To calculate the current draw of these, simply add the numbers to the equation:

Current = 120W/12V = 10A

This means that, technically, a 10-amp cable would be sufficient to supply the socket. However, it is good practice to provide some head room when cable sizing, so a 17-amp cable would work better.

CABLE SELECTION

One of the most important aspects of designing and building a camper van electrical system is deciding on the correct size and type of cable to use for each circuit. Current draw is not the only factor to consider. If you choose a cable that is too small, there is a risk of generating too much heat in the cable; if it is too large, you will be wasting money on copper (which is essentially what you are paying for when you buy cable).

Cable Construction

The cables used in vehicle electrical systems are very flexible in contrast to the cabling found in domestic building wiring, which is fairly stiff. The reason for this is that copper is ductile, but is susceptible to 'work hardening' when subject to vibration and mechanical shock. Obviously, the cable in a house wall never moves, but wires in a camper van experience a whole host of vibrations, from the engine, the road surface and other sources. This work hardening causes the metal to become brittle, which could, over a long period of time, cause the conductor to crack.

This problem is overcome by manufacturing the core from many small-diameter strands of copper wire to make up the desired cross-sectional area, rather than using a single wire. This type of cable is known as 'stranded' cable and provides much more flexibility. The improved resistance to work hardening makes it better suited to use in vehicles.

Cable Specifications

Most cable that you buy, whether from a motor factors or online retailer, will have its specification written either on the insulation or on the cable reel. However, different terms are sometimes used to describe the cable's properties and these can be a little confusing to the uninitiated. Depending on the supplier, a cable will have a combination of the following details in its specification:

- Cross-sectional area: expressed in mm^2, this refers to the total cross-sectional area of the copper conductor. Cable is sometimes described as '1mm' or '2mm', without the ^{2} sign, but it is important to note that this does not mean the diameter of the cable. This can often lead to confusion – remember that the main specification for a cable will be its conductor's cross-sectional area and cable will never be referred to by its diameter alone.
- Conductor number and size: expressed as the number of conductors of a given diameter. So 28/0.30 means that there are 28 strands, each with a diameter of 0.30mm
- Nominal current rating: expressed in amperes (amps or A), the maximum continuous or 'working' current that the cable can safely carry.
- Overall diameter: the diameter of the cable expressed in mm, not to be confused with cross-sectional area.
- Resistance: expressed in ohms per metre, this specification is useful for working out the voltage drop along a wire.

The information provided in the specification will help you decide which cable is needed for a particular application.

Calculating Suitable Cable Size

There are a number of factors that need to be taken into consideration when selecting cable.

The first factor to look at will be the current draw of the component you are connecting. Each component connected to a circuit will have a particular current draw, which can be calculated using the relevant equation (*see* page 98). It is important that the cable supplying power to each component is capable of carrying the normally expected current, plus a margin of safety. If it is not capable then the most likely problem is that the cable may heat up and potentially catch fire. While all circuits should be fused, with the fuse blowing before the safe working current of the particular circuit is exceeded, it is important to ensure that cables have sufficient current-carrying capacity not to over-heat under normal use.

electricity

A good multi-meter is invaluable.

The second electrical phenomenon to consider when calculating cable size is voltage drop. Even cables have a resistance, meaning there will be a loss of energy as power is transmitted along it, resulting in a voltage drop. Just as a light bulb converts electrical energy to light and heat through its wire filament, so does a cable. This means that, if there is excessive resistance in a cable compared to the voltage running along it, insufficient power will be provided to the component that it is supposed to supply. This is a particular problem in 12V vehicle wiring systems, where there is not much voltage to start with. Even relatively short cable runs can result in a voltage drop. A clear example of this can be found in very old vehicles that only have 6V electrics. Very often, the headlights are not much better than candles, as the resistance provided by old cables and dirty connections means that you are lucky if as many as 4 volts actually reach the bulb.

The answer is to ensure that the cables used to connect components are large enough to limit voltage drop to within acceptable limits. To continue with the plumbing analogy, the larger the cable, the less resistance it will have to current flowing along it. An acceptable level of voltage drop is generally taken as 3 per cent. Using the equation of V = IR, the voltage drop for a particular circuit may be calculated, provided the current draw of the component being supplied and the resistance of the cable are known. With automotive cable, this is normally written on the side and expressed in ohms/metre.

Using the example of the 12V socket, which has a known current draw of 10A, it is possible to calculate the size of cable that is needed in order to obtain an acceptable voltage. For example, looking at a $0.5mm^2$ cable (rated at 11A) that has a resistance of 0.037 ohms/metre, and a cable run to the socket of 5m, the calculation would be as follows:

Voltage drop = amps (I) × Resistance (R) = 10A × (5 × 0.037 ohms) = 1.85V

This drop of 1.85 volts is 15 per cent, significantly over the allowable limit.

However, looking at a $3mm^2$ cable rated to 25A with a resistance of 0.006 ohms/metre, the calculation would be as follows:

Voltage drop = amps (I) × Resistance (R) = 10A × (5x 0.0006 ohms) = 0.3V

The percentage voltage drop = 100 × (0.3/12) = 2.5 per cent, which is nicely within the 3 per cent allowable limit.

If for some reason your cable does not have its resistance written on the insulation, it is quite easy to work it out using the following rough guide. A $1.0mm^2$ cable will have a resistance of approximately 18.1 ohms per 1,000m. Therefore, 1m of such a cable has a resistance of 0.0181 ohms (18.1/1,000). Knowing this measurement, it is easy to scale up and down, so a $2mm^2$ cable has double the conductor area and thus half the resistance, at 9.05 ohms per 1,000m or 0.009 ohms/metre. A $1.5mm^2$ cable has 50 per cent more conductor area, so divide 18.1 by 1.5, giving 12.06 ohms per 1,000m, or 0.012 ohms/m.

Although this maths may seem intimidating, once you get used to it, calculating cable sizes is very straightforward and will help prevent any problems with cables getting overloaded. However, if in doubt, it is always best to over- rather than under-size a cable, just to be on the safe side.

MAKING JOINTS

Crimping

Tip: be careful when stripping the insulation from a stranded cable that you do not accidentally remove any of the copper strands. This will reduce the total cross-sectional area of the conductor at that point and consequently also reduce the current-carrying capacity of the cable. The same applies when crimping the conductor to a terminal – make sure all strands are crimped or the current-carrying capacity will be reduced.

Ratchet crimp tools.

Basic wiring tools.

Soldering

There are a host of different ways of joining cables, including 'chocolate block' and crimp-type connectors, but a soldered joint is by far and away the best approach. A properly soldered joint is incredibly durable, takes up little space and looks very neat. It may take a little longer than a simple crimp, but in the long run it will provide a far more pleasing solution.

There are a number of different soldering-iron options available. Basic 240V models can be inexpensive, however, the cheapest versions are not all that durable and tend to burn out quickly. For most wiring work a small 30W iron will suffice, providing plenty of heat for all but the largest-gauge wiring. Another option is to use a non-electric iron – essentially a small blow torch that uses butane fuel and can be used with either a naked flame or heated tip. Although it will be slightly more expensive than a plug-in unit, it will provide great versatility and its small size and lack of a cord mean that you can get into tight spaces, making it ideal for the confines of a bus. A power-adjustable model will allow you to vary the temperature of the tip. This is a useful feature, especially if joining very thin wiring, but it is not vital.

Although it may be stating the obvious, soldering irons get very hot. You must take precautions not to set your pride and joy on fire (tempting though it may be after chasing a wiring fault for several hours) and do not touch the hot end!

For a really professional job, it is best to use heat-shrink tubing to insulate the joints after soldering. This can be bought in multi packs containing short lengths of varying diameters, or by the metre from most motor factors. Electrical tape will do the job but it looks messy and does not provide the same level of protection.

Strip the cable ends.

When it comes to stripping, a dedicated wire-stripping tool will make removing the insulation from cables a doddle. However, careful use of side cutters will also fulfil the same role. When using the strippers, one side of the tool grips the wire, while the other cuts through the insulation and pulls it off as the tool opens. It is important to be careful when stripping wires not to remove any of the wire itself, as this will reduce the current-handling ability.

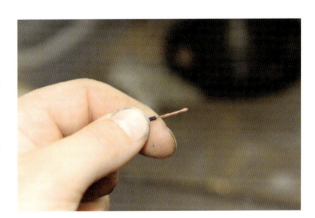
Twist the strands tightly together.

electricity

Once you have stripped the end off the cable, twist the strands together nice and tightly. Although it looks like this will mean the solder will only sit on the outside of the wire, it will easily run between the strands.

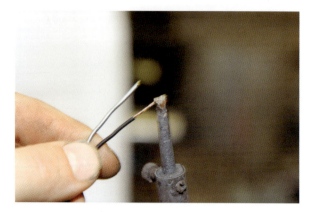

'Tin' the cable ends.

Attaching a Connector on to a Cable

When attaching a connector on to a cable, to allow the solder to take nicely, it is best to 'tin' the end of the wire before putting it in the connector. This involves putting a very small quantity of solder on to the wire's tip. Heat the wire with the soldering iron, then just touch the solder to the wire – It should be hot enough to melt and will run freely between the strands.

Fit the connector and heat the solder.

Then, add the connector. Ring connectors are ideal for creating earth connections to the body work for items such as lights and stereos. Slide the heat-shrink tubing over the wire (it will not fit on after the connector is attached), then poke the tinned wire into the connector so it just extends out of the end. Now, heat both the connector and the wire with the iron. You will know when it is hot enough because the solder will flow freely, with capillary action drawing it into the barrel of the connector. Add enough solder to fill the barrel and secure the wire.

The finished connector with heat-shrink tubing applied.

You should end up with a super solid connection that will conduct well and last a long time. The final stage is to shrink the heat-shrink. Pull the tube so that it is covering the barrel of the connector – this not only insulates it, but also provides support for the cable at the joint, where it is most likely to fail over time. The tubing can be shrunk with a hot-air gun or even just a butane lighter (although if you are using any colour other than black you will end up with sooty marks).

Twist two cables together and heat the wire before adding solder.

Splicing Two Wires Together

Splicing is ideal if you want to put a neat repair into a faulty section of wiring and it is not practical to replace the whole wire. First, strip about 15–20mm of insulation off each cable. Next, hold the cable together and twist the ends around each other, trying to twist each wire equally. At this point, remember to slide a bit of heat-shrink on to the cable. Note that the overall diameter of the twisted cable is not greater than the cable insulation. If you do not twist each wire equally, you can end up with lumps and bumps that can pierce the heat-shrink insulation, leading to short circuits. Using the same technique as you do for tinning the single cable, heat the wire and let the solder run between the strands. You do not need to use a lot of solder and it should just cover all of the wire strands. When cool, this provides a nice solid joint, however, it is not as flexible as the wire on its own so try to place the joints where they can run in straight line.

Shrink on the sleeving and you should have a wonderfully neat and, more importantly, reliable joint that will last for ever.

A neat and insulated cable joint.

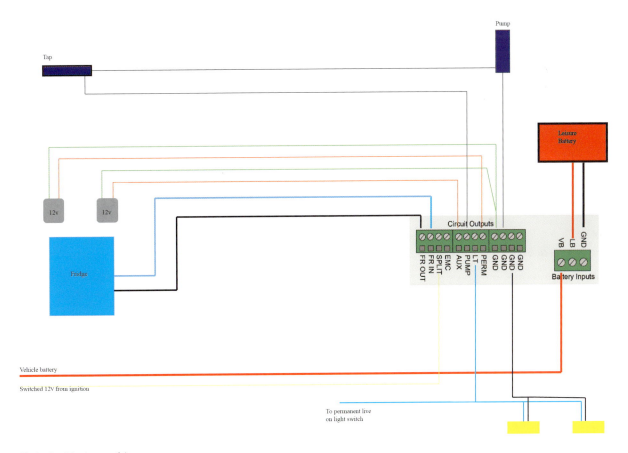

The basic wiring layout of the van.

electricity

THE VAN INSTALLATION

Wiring for Appliances

Measure the length of the kitchen unit.

Fix the conduit to the van.

In our van all the wiring for the fridge and charger sockets was to be run behind the cupboard units, with the power-management system (PMS) housed in the cupboard under the sink.

The conduit was screwed to the side of the van, terminating in the centre of the enclosure for the fridge. The trim panels under the carpet were located and screwed into with regular wood screws – a lot easier than trying to screw into the bodywork.

Wiring conduit is available from vendors such as Screwfix.

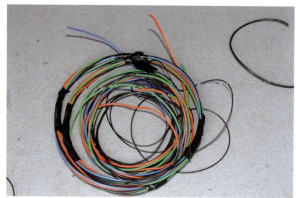

The wiring loom ready for fitting.

The first job was to measure the distance from the location of the PMS to the end of the cupboards. To keep the wiring tidy, it was decided to house it in simple white plastic cable conduit, which can be purchased very cheaply in 2m lengths from any electrical suppliers. It has a snap-on top cover, so that the wires can be placed in the conduit and the cover snapped on, saving the hassle of trying to feed wires along it.

Using the appropriate calculations (*see* page 99), the correct sizes of cable were selected for each appliance. The fridge is fused at 15 amps but a 21A cable was used, to give a little head room. The sockets are rated at 120W, so, given a 12V supply, they need a minimum of 10A cable; a 17.5A wire was used to give a safety margin. The tap (which connects to the submersible pump) was wired with 11A cable.

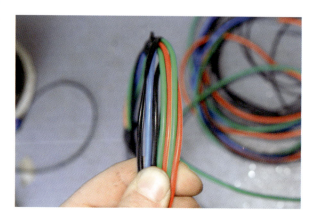

Colour coding makes life a lot easier.

electricity

Colour coding of the cables helps keep track of what does what. In this installation, the green and red wires supply the 12V sockets, the thick blue and black the fridge, while the thin black wires are for the tap.

Quick-disconnect battery terminals are a good idea.

Feed the cables into the conduit.

The 125Ah leisure battery in its box.

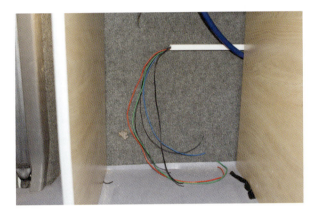

Leave plenty of spare cable.

Do not finally cut the wiring to length until it is fed into the conduit. Also, ensure that the wires are not packed too tightly into the conduit as this could lead to over-heating. We placed about the maximum number of wires into our 16mm conduit; if there had been additional appliances, it would have been sensible to move up to a 25mm conduit. It should also be noted here that the feed to the front vehicle battery is not run in the conduit, as this may get warm when the charger is operating.

Once all the wires are in place, cut them to length, ensuring that they are not pulled tight at any point. The result should be a very neat cable installation that does not look like a bird's nest.

Another integral part of the electrical system is the leisure battery. Having a leisure battery means that you can run all of your electrical systems without fear of running down your main battery, which might leave you stranded. Leisure batteries are generally available from most caravan stores, with outputs ranging from 85Ah to 125Ah; the larger the capacity, the longer they will last.

Some people choose to fit multiple batteries, but we opted for only one as the conversion will not be particularly power-hungry. The battery was installed in the void between the bed and the wheel arch. It is important for the battery to be secured well and, ideally, housed in a dedicated battery box. The box, which has a lid that fits over the top, was screwed securely to the floor.

The Sergant EC160 power-management system.

electricity

The EC160 fitted under the cooker unit.

Power-Management System

The power-management system is the part that controls all of the leisure electrics, looking after the 240V and 12V vehicle and leisure batteries. There are a number of units available on the market and your choice depends on your needs. If you are only running a 12V system, a unit such as the Zig CP400 can be used, which costs about £70. However, for 12/240V installations, a more complex controller is needed. One popular choice is the Zig CF9, but for this van we chose to use the lesser-known Sergant EC160.

The benefit of this set-up is that is has everything contained in one box, including the circuit breakers for the 240V side of the system. (If you run a Zig unit, a separate 240V consumer unit is needed to ensure safe operation of any 240V equipment.)

The EC160 specification is as follows:

- 230V AC 16A input via pre-wired 2m lead, RCD protected with reverse polarity indication. Built-in 150W 13.8V fixed voltage battery charger with on/off switch, 3 × 10A MCB outputs via quick-fit connector blocks.
- 12V DC 2 × 15A battery inputs via screw terminal block.
- 5 × outputs via screw terminal block: pump output via pump switch and 5A fuse; lights output via lights/aux switch and lights 10A fuse; aux output via lights/aux switch and aux 10A fuse; permanent output via 5A fuse; fridge output via 15A fuse.
- Built-in split charge relay (configurable).
- Built-in EMC isolation relay (configurable).
- Digital voltmeter with on/off switch.
- Dimensions: front panel 300 × 150mm, panel cut-out 285 × 132mm, depth 200mm.

Installation of the unit is fairly straightforward, provided you proceed in a logical fashion. The first decision is where to site the unit. After a bit of thought, we settled on the cupboard under the cooker unit, which would provide a good balance between accessibility and aesthetics. Some conversions site the unit in full view, but this is not a very attractive approach.

To operate a split charge system, you need to run a cable from the main vehicle battery to the PMS. If you are running a traditional split charge, which uses a separate relay to directly link the vehicle and leisure batteries when the vehicle is running, it is necessary to use a very heavy-duty cable. A flat leisure battery can draw a lot of current when left to its own devices. The split charger in the EC160 is more intelligent than that and limits the charging current to 15 amps, so a smaller cable can be used. In our van we opted for a 2mm cable to account for the voltage drop over the run from the battery to the rear of the van.

To fit the cable, we simply removed the scuttle panel from the engine bay and ran the cable across to the driver's side, where there was an obvious grommet to access the interior. Once through this grommet, we ran the cable under the cab floor mat and behind the interior units. This cable will connect to the terminal on the unit marked 'vehicle battery'. Meanwhile, the cable from the leisure battery will connect to the terminal marked 'leisure battery'. The final connection will be to earth.

For the rest of the connections, you simply need to attach the wiring you have already installed to the relevant plugs. On our van, we chose to make the front-most 12V socket a permanent live (as long as the PMS itself is switched on), meaning it is always available to charge items such as telephones. For advice on installing the sockets, *see* later in this chapter; after the sockets have been installed, attaching the 240V wiring from them is reasonably straightforward. Remember the standard European wiring and connect each wire to the relevant connector on the PMS (all are very clearly labelled):

- Live – brown;
- Earth – yellow and green;
- Neutral – blue.

Feed from the vehicle battery is routed through the driver's-side scuttle grommet.

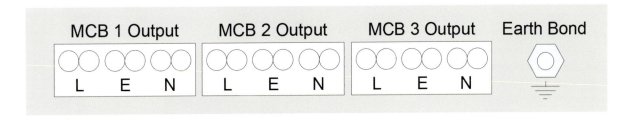

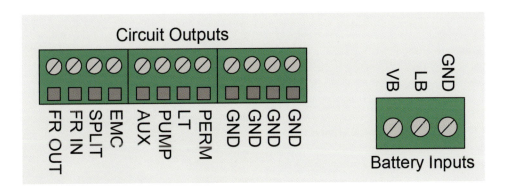

Wiring connector layout on the EC160.

Simple screw terminals are easy to use.

Tidy the wiring with cable ties.

Finally, make sure that all of your earth connections are in place. The most important is the earth from the PMS to the vehicle body. This means that if there is a short circuit in the system, the electricity has an earth path back to the circuit breaker on the mains. If this is not installed and there is a fault in the vehicle wiring, the most likely earth path will be you when you touch the bodywork.

MAINS CONNECTION

A 240V mains hook-up is a very handy addition if you intend to spend any length of time at a campsite. It means that you can keep your leisure battery charged while still utilizing all of your 12V connections, while also allowing you to run 240V appliances such as kettles and even toasters! Fitting a supply is very easy, but any 240V installation really should be tested and signed off by a suitably qualified electrician. Even if you fit all of the wiring yourself, it is worth getting it checked by a pro, as the consequences of a faulty set-up can be fatal.

electricity

> ### CONNECTING SAFELY TO A MAINS SUPPLY
>
> For your safety it is important that you follow these connection instructions each time your camper is connected to a mains supply. This section assumes that the system is complete and that a leisure battery has been installed.
>
> 1. **Ensure suitability of the mains supply.** Your leisure vehicle should only be connected to an approved supply that meets the requirements of BS7671 or relevant harmonized standards. In most cases the site warden will hold information regarding suitability of supply. If using a generator you also need to comply with the requirements/instructions supplied with the generator. Please note that some electronic generators may not be compatible with your leisure system.
> 2. **Switch the power supply unit internal battery charger off.** Locate the battery charger power switch on the PSU and ensure the switch is in the off position (switch up) before connection to the mains supply.
> 3. **Connect the hook-up lead.** First, connect the hook-up lead (orange cable with blue connectors) to the leisure vehicle and then connect to the mains supply.
> 4. **Check residual current device operation.** Locate the RCD within the PSU and ensure the RCD is switched on (lever in up position). Press the 'Test' button and confirm that the RCD turns off (lever in down position). Switch the RCD back to the on position (lever in up position). If the test button fails to operate the RCD, check the mains supply.
> 5. **Check miniature circuit breakers.** Locate the MCBs within the PSU (adjacent to the RCD) and ensure they are all in the on (up) position. If any MCB fails to 'latch' in the on position seek expert help.
> 6. **Turn the PSU on.** Locate the battery select switch (Vehicle/Leisure) and switch to the leisure position to select the leisure battery. If the installation is in a motorhome or caravan with the car attached, then the switch can be moved to the vehicle position to use the vehicle battery if required. Now locate the battery charger switch and switch to the on position. The battery charger will now start to charge the selected battery.
> 7. **Check correct polarity.** Locate the 'Reverse Polarity' indicator on the PSU and ensure that the indicator is *not* illuminated. If the indicator is illuminated this could be caused by a reversed supply, portable generator being used or faulty hook-up cable. In this case, expert advice should be sought.
> 8. **Check operation of equipment.** It is now safe to operate the 12V and 230V equipment. Depending on how the system has been wired, the lights/aux switch with turn on/off the lighting circuit (this switch is often used as the master lights switch) and the auxiliary circuit (which is often used for 12V sockets, TV amplifier, heater and oven igniter and so on). The pump switch is used to turn on/off the water pump (and also in many cases the toilet flush pump).

Reimo 240V terminal.

The standard 3-pin female 240V connection.

Screw down wiring terminals to the rear.

On a standard set-up, the power lead from the mains hooks into the caravan/camper van 240V connection, which in turn is connected to the PMS. Under the flip-up cover is a 3-pin plug with a retaining clip to prevent the cable being pulled loose. At the rear of the unit are three connections – live, neutral and earth – exactly as you would find in a household plug.

electricity

Mark the location of the socket.

Use a large hole saw to cut out the centre, then trim with a hacksaw blade.

Many conversions feature the mains connection in the side of the van. However, we felt that this would be rather unsightly; it also requires considerable cutting of the bodywork and could potentially lead to rust problems further down the line. Many older campers come into the VWorks premises with rust holes around the mains plugs. When undertaking conversions for a major conversion company, Sam Jeffery had previously relocated the connection to the rear quarter panel, so this was the approach we decided to take. There is a large space behind the trim panel below the rear light, which can easily accommodate the socket. Start by removing the rear light and carefully unclipping the trim panel; it is located on tabs and to remove it the panel must be slid up and over the boot lid stay (the lump on the left-hand side).

Once you have decided on the exact location of the socket, apply plenty of masking tape to the surrounding area to protect it. We used a large hole saw to start the hole before finishing it with a jigsaw, all the while being careful not to damage the paint finish.

Refit and mark the inner panel.

With the panel refitted it was possible to check where the backing plate would need cutting. This is attached using small (and very delicate) plastic poppers similar to those used to secure the interior trim panels. With these removed we trimmed a hole to accommodate the rear of the plug box.

Remove the cover panel and mask it up.

Drill through to the interior of the van.

electricity

Be sure to use grommets to prevent the sharp metal cutting the cable.

Route the mains cable behind the carpet lining.

It was then necessary to drill through the bodywork in order to route the cable into the van. This was done using a stepped drill bit. There are four layers of panel work to go through in total, so take your time. It is imperative that the mains cable is protected from the resulting sharp edges so rubber grommets were added. It is nigh-on impossible to get grommets on the inner panel skins, so instead the cable was sheathed in a spare section of water hose and then threaded through the holes. Once the cable had been fed through the bodywork it was then encased under the carpet, appearing inside the rear cupboard unit ready for connection to the PMS.

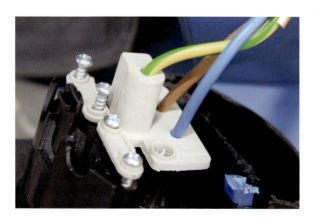

Remember the colours for the connections: Brown – live, Blue – neutral, Yellow/Green – earth.

The final task was to connect the cable to the socket: brown to positive, blue to neutral and yellow/green to earth. The socket was then secured to the trim panel using small self-tapping screws. The result is a mains hook-up that is far less conspicuous than it would be if it had been located in the side of the van.

FITTING INTERIOR SOCKETS

Place the socket surround in the desired location.

Find the centre point of the socket surround.

You can never have too many interior electrical sockets, so fit as many as your PMS will accommodate. The sockets used in our van, produced by a company called CBE, are designed specifically for camper and caravan use and have matching surrounds for both 12V and 240V sockets. As with most accessories, they can be purchased from any decent caravan suppliers. Fitting them to your interior units is an easy task, requiring the use of a hole saw and a steady hand.

electricity

Carefully cut with a hole saw.

Ensure the socket is square and fix with small screws.

Some extra sanding may be needed for a perfect fit.

The finished item looks factory-fitted.

Once you have decided on the location of the various sockets, remove the surrounds and offer them up to the surface where you wish to mount them. Draw around the socket and determine the centre point. For the 12V sockets we had chosen, a 1½-in (38-mm) hole saw was required. Working carefully, so as not to chip the veneer, we cut out a hole for the socket to sit in. It may be necessary to add additional clearance to accommodate the exact shape of the socket.

Once the socket fits neatly in the hole, remove the surrounding cover and ensure that the unit is sitting level – as it is not the same colour as the light wood furniture, any misalignment will be easy to spot. Use four small self-tapping screws to secure the socket in place, ensure that the screws have a small head otherwise they may interfere with the cover.

A double socket is a little trickier to mark out.

Place the socket in the hole.

electricity

The sockets came supplied with cable tails.

Ensure the holes are level.

The protective backing cover prevents accidents and removes any need for boxing in.

Cable tails can be hidden in trunking or simply cable-tied out of the way.

The 240V sockets are fitted in a very similar fashion, but require a slightly different approach, due to their greater bulk. Our sockets were supplied with pre-terminated cables, although they can be purchased without cables. Use the same approach for marking out the mounting – this time, the holes will measure 52mm in diameter because of the larger back cover that the socket has to accommodate the 240V wiring.

With 240V sockets the sky is the limit.

With the holes drilled, clean up the edges to prevent the veneer chipping. As these are double sockets, each individual plug needs to be located precisely in order for the cover to fit on correctly. It is here that accurate marking pays off; if it has been done correctly, the cover should clip straight on. Thanks to the built-in protective covers, there is no need to box in the backs of the sockets and all that remains is to route the cables and connect them to the PMS.

The Sargent unit that we used in our van does not accept the quick connectors fitted to the cables, so these needed to be cut off and the wires stripped to fit the PMS. Strip about 10mm of insulation off the wires and connect blue to neutral, yellow and green to earth and brown to live. Then you are ready to put the kettle on, or the microwave, or even a TV!

INTERIOR LIGHTS

Where you choose to place interior lights is very much a matter of personal choice. For our conversion we chose to keep things simple, with three LED downlighters, two above the kitchen unit and one above the door. These were sourced from IKEA, with a set of four costing around £20.

The intention was to make the lights operate along with the door opening lights, yet also run off the leisure battery supply. In order to do this, a three-way switch was needed. VW provides the ideal candidate – a standard front interior light found in any T5 or other similar vintage VW has a three-way switch integrated into it. This allows for switching between the standard interior light circuit and the leisure battery.

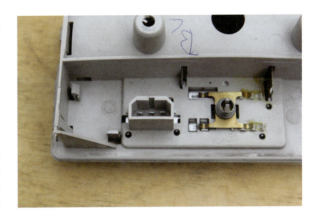

Three-pin connector with permanent live, ignition live and ground.

Using a multi-meter, identify which wire is the permanent live and which is switched off as the doors are closed or the ignition switched on. The permanent feed will be replaced by the feed from your leisure battery. The reasons for this are twofold. First, you do not want to drain your vehicle battery with the lights (although LED lights do have a very low current draw). Second, even the permanent feed features a timer, so after about 15 minutes your lights would switch off, requiring a door to be opened to turn them back on.

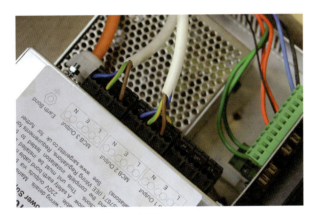

Wiring into the EC160 is straightforward.

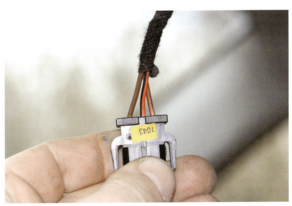

Try to find a VW plug to utilize; the second-hand switch used here came with one fitted.

The standard VW front light fitting.

electricity

Trim the light section leaving just the switch.

The four-way splitter on the Ikea lights.

To create a switch from the interior light unit, some judicious use of a hacksaw is required to remove the lighting portion of the unit. The switch section can then be mounted into the ceiling of the van in a position of your choice. As you are working with LED, which only works with current running one way, you will need to identify which is the negative connection of the prongs of the light (that would normally hold the bulb). Either solder wire tails to these prongs or trim them so that they will accept a crimp. From the switch, the wiring is fed through a small voltage regulator, incorporated into the light unit junction box. This is necessary because LEDs can blow very easily if subjected to too high a voltage and the voltage supplied by the vehicle battery can reach up to 13.5V.

With all the wiring connected, it can be hidden up above the roof lining out of the way, and the lights can be positioned where you want them.

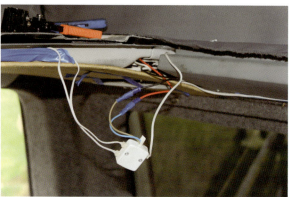

Wiring can be tucked under a headlining panel.

The lights were attached using self-adhesive Velcro.

Wiring diagram for the interior lighting circuit.

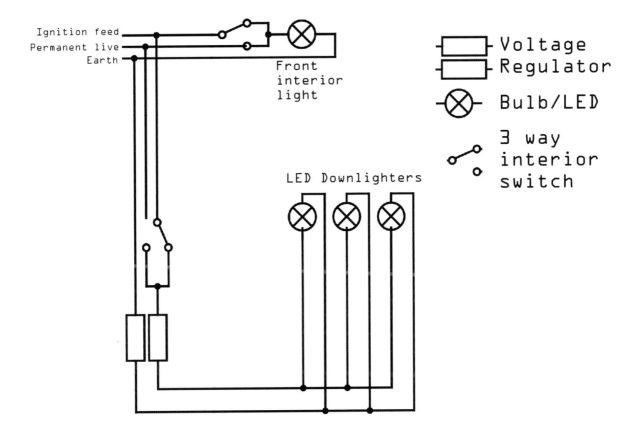

9

useful extras

Unless you have purchased a particularly posh specification of new T5, it is more than likely that you will not have desirable extras such as a factory-fitted satellite navigation system or reversing camera/sensors. Fortunately, the price of such technology is falling all of the time and, if you are willing to avoid the big brand names, you can retro-fit your van for surprisingly little money.

STEREO UNIT

For several years now the internet has been awash with no-brand Chinese car stereos and other equipment. Following some research, it appeared that some of these set-ups were worth further investigation. The requirement was for a 'double DIN'-sized stereo unit, capable of playing DVDs, accepting an MP3 player input and incorporating a satellite navigation system.

The stereo we opted for was sourced from an online vendor, with the choice being based on a combination of aesthetics, functionality and user feedback. The unit features a built-in multi-region DVD player, a video input, video output as well as two phono outputs and an phono input. It all runs on Windows' CE mobile operating system, which has a proven track record of being (relatively) reliable. We also sourced a wireless reversing camera system from another vendor. This came in a kit that consisted of a camera unit, a wireless transmitter and a receiver, which simply plugs into an available video input on the chosen head unit. The stereo and camera were obtained for a combined cost of less than £200.

Remove the standard single or double radio.

The radio and camera system was sourced online from a Chinese seller.

The VW aerial connector.

> **'DOUBLE DIN'**
>
> 'Double DIN' refers to the size of the radio-mounting aperture and not the front panel, as some people mistakenly think. Originally established by the German standards body Deutsches Institut für Normung, as DIN 75490, the standard defines car audio head units and enclosures and is therefore commonly referred to as the 'DIN car radio size'. It was adopted as International Standard ISO 7736 in 1984. Head units generally come in either single DIN (180 × 50mm panel) or double DIN (180 × 100mm panel) size. The US market uses measurements of 2 × 7in or 4 × 7in.

useful extras

Adaptor to fit DIN-type radios.

Release the floor mat from the door seal.

The first task is to remove the standard stereo. Depending on the year of van you have, this may be a single DIN tape player, with a storage compartment above, or a double DIN CD unit. You will need a set of removal keys, which can be purchased from most motor factors for a few pounds. If you have a single unit with a storage compartment, this simply unclips once the stereo is removed. The standard VW radio features two ISO multi-plugs, one for power and the second for audio. The new radio came with an adaptor to allow these plugs to be fitted to the new unit, which uses a DIN standard plug. The same applies to the radio connection, so an ISO to DIN aerial adaptor is required.

Video and audio cable for rear compartment.

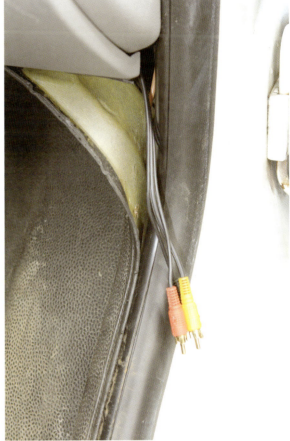

Feed the cable through.

Remove the cab step cover.

The new radio is capable of playing DVDs as well as videos from a memory card, although it would be nigh-on impossible to see the 7-in screen from a seat in the back of the van. Taking advantage of the fact that the head unit features video and audio outputs, we decided to run a video cable to the rear of the van, allowing for the future fitment of a video screen when budgets allows. It is quite simple, if a little fiddly, to secrete the cable. To begin with it was fed down the right-hand side of the stereo aperture and underneath the instrument column. A piece of stiff wire with a hook bent in the end was used to snare it through the gap at the bottom of the steering column, and it was then fed

useful extras

along to the far right-hand side of the dashboard. It is possible to remove the lower dash panel, but this seemed like the easier approach.

We then removed the plastic doorstep cover and pulled the rubber floor matting away from the door seal, being careful not to tear it. The step cover can be tough to remove, as it has adhesive underneath, but a sharp tug should do the trick. It was then simply a matter of routing the cable across the door threshold, under the rear door trim and behind the interior units. When the time comes to fit a screen in the rear, it will be very simple to plug it in. Alternatively, the two audio connectors could be attached to an amplifier to power rear speakers or a sub-woofer.

The stereo had a wiring diagram attached, which made life easier.

Remove the dash-top storage tray.

Drill a hole and feed the auxiliary cable through.

Conveniently, the radio had a schematic of the connections printed on top of it, making it easy to put the right plugs in the right place. There is a dashboard reinforcement directly behind the radio, so, depending on how many devices you are attaching, things may become a little cramped. This reinforcement piece is only made of plastic and can be trimmed out of the way if necessary.

The video camera, video and power connectors.

The green wire is the reversing-light feed.

Although the head unit is able to accept an i-Pod interface, you may want to add a regular 3.5mm audio input jack, so that you can use different types of music player. The head unit did not have an input on the front, so instead a phono to 3.5mm jack cable was used, connected to the radio's audio input sockets. The ideal place to keep a music device seemed to be the dash-top storage tray, so a hole was drilled in one of the compartments to allow the cable to pass through. A small hole was also drilled on the front-most edge of the tray for the GPS aerial cable, which sits at the very front of the windscreen, where it can see the sky.

REVERSING CAMERA

You may not always need a reversing camera, but you will be grateful for it when it helps you avoid that short post that is just out of view in the mirrors. It is relatively straightforward to fit, consisting of a transmitter/power unit and a camera unit that connect together. The camera is fitted into the rear bumper just above the towbar (handy for reversing), while the transmitter is housed just under the N/S rear light cluster. Power for the camera is taken from the green reversing-light cable (on a 2004-spec T5), meaning that it will only power up when the vehicle is put in reverse. The power lead from the camera is spliced into the vehicle harness, while the earth is attached to an earthing point that was fitted for the towbar electrics.

Carefully drill a hole for the camera.

Position the camera in the desired position.

Check the orientation of the image.

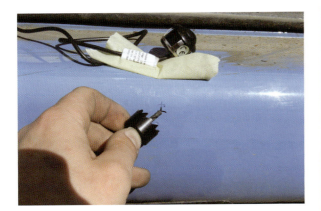

Mark a central point.

To start with, the camera system was mocked up in place to check how much the towbar ball would interfere with the field of view. In order to do this, the head unit was plugged in and powered up, and the WiFi receiver attached to the video input. The vehicle was put in reverse and the picture checked. Once we were happy with the location of the camera, a 25mm hole was drilled in the bumper, taking care not to make it oversized, and the camera was slotted into the hole. It was held in place by a small metal spring collar.

The wireless sender unit was secured behind the trim panel.

useful extras

With the camera in place, the image needed orienting. The camera mount is like a ball and socket, and the image can be rotated 360 degrees; unfortunately, there was no marking for 'top dead centre', so someone needed to sit in the van and direct the person at the rear to rotate the camera until the image was level.

Once everything was working correctly, the wiring was routed through a convenient hole between the bumper and the rear-quarter trim and the WiFi transmitter secured in place with cable ties. All of the cable connections were also wrapped in waterproof tape – although the camera claimed to be rated to IP67 (the top rating for weather resistance), the connections most certainly were not, so this extra precaution seemed like a good idea.

The fully functioning hi-tech stereo.

Insert the cage for the stereo.

Foam blocks help prevent movement.

With all of the wiring in place, all that remained was to fit the securing cage for the stereo. This slides into the aperture and is secured in place by tabs that bend out to interlock with the back of the dash. Self-adhesive foam pads supplied with the radio help secure the unit and damp out any potential rattles, and there was also a facia panel to finish the installation off neatly. The whole fitting process, for both the camera and radio, took about two hours. Considering the price of the parts, it represented a very worthwhile improvement in terms of both entertainment and practicality.

TOWBAR

Options

A towbar can be a very useful addition to any van – not only can you pull a trailer, or even a caravan, it can also be used to attach accessories such as a bike rack. A factory-fitted towbar was a very expensive option, so few vans left the dealer with one; however, retro-fitting is an easy task. There are many different types of towbar available, with options such as a fixed or removable hitch. We opted for a very basic bar and, because our van was being built on a limited budget, we sourced it second-hand.

In the past, fitting the wiring needed for a towbar could be a bit challenging, but today there are plenty of companies that supply vehicle-specific wiring kits for the T5, so connecting everything up is a cinch. It goes without saying that the most important stage of the fitting process is ensuring the bar is attached securely – tighten those nuts! The last thing you want is your trailer, hitch and all, parting company from the van at speed.

useful extras

> **RULES AND REGULATIONS: WHAT YOU CAN TOW**
>
> There are rules governing who can tow what and how heavy it can be. The following information is taken from the gov.uk website.
>
> **Licences issued from 19 January 2013**
>
> From 19 January 2013, drivers passing a category B (car and small vehicle) test can tow:
>
> Small trailers weighing no more than 750kg.
> Trailers weighing more than 750kg, where the combined weight of the towing vehicle and the trailer is not more than 3,500kg.
>
> If you want to tow a trailer weighing more than 750kg, when the combined weight of the towing vehicle and trailer is more than 3,500kg, you will have to pass a further test and get B+E entitlement on your licence. You will then be able to tow trailers up to 3,500kg.
>
> **Licences held from 1 January 1997**
>
> If you passed your driving test after 1 January 1997 and have an ordinary category B (car) licence, you can drive either:
>
> A vehicle up to 3.5 tonnes or 3,500kg Maximum Authorised Mass (MAM) towing a trailer of up to 750kg MAM (with a combined weight of up to 4,250kg in total).
> A trailer over 750kg MAM as long as it is no more than the unladen weight of the towing vehicle (with a combined weight of up to 3,500kg in total).
>
> **Licences held before 1 January 1997**
>
> If you passed your car test before 1 January 1997 you are generally entitled to drive a vehicle and trailer combination up to 8.25 tonnes MAM. This is the weight of a vehicle or trailer including the maximum load that can be carried safely when it is being used on the road. You also have entitlement to drive a minibus with a trailer over 750kg MAM.

Fitting

The towbar wiring kit that was sourced online.

The towbar mount.

Our vehicle-specific wiring kit was purchased online, mainly because it was cheap. It turned out to be made by Westfalia; it was top quality and included every part we needed. The towbar was also sourced online second-hand – if you buy a second-hand item, make sure you get all of the fixing bolts with the bar.

Remove the rear light units.

Trim clips are the same awful design as the interior panels.

useful extras

In order to fit the bar, it is necessary to remove the bumper, so the first job is to unscrew the rear lights. As you will be playing with the electrics, it is also a good idea to disconnect the battery. With the lights out of the way, remove the corner covers. These are held in place by Allen-head plastic fixings. These can be a pain to remove as the socket rounds off very easily. A good tip is to use a slightly oversized imperial Allen key.

Behind the cover is another plastic panel, which clips into the top of the bumper. This needs to be removed too. Move round to the inner arches and remove the lower two screws on the arch liner. They are Torx head, so make sure you have the right set of driver bits. Two of these are tricky to find – if you pull the arch liner out of the way you will find a pair of screws hidden behind it.

The black trim panel must also be removed.

The spare wheel needs to be released in order to access the central mounting tab.

The arch lining is secured with torx screws.

Drop the rear undertray out of the way.

Bumper screws are hidden behind the lining.

Under the bumper are three fixing tabs, only two of which have screws in them. Remove these and drop the spare wheel while you are at it. (This is a good time to check that you can actually undo the spare-wheel nuts. Ours were seized solid, which we would not want to find out when trying to sort out a puncture on a cold winter's night!) With a bit of jiggling, the bumper cover will simply pull off. If it refuses to come, double-check you have got all of the screws out. Most vans will have a plastic undertray, held in with a variety of 10mm and 13mm bolts plus a couple of screws. Remove these and drop it out of the way. This will provide access to the chassis legs.

The bumper is secured by four large bolts on either side.

Get the rear bolts fixed first.

The cavity into which the towbar mount will slide.

The towbar has captive nuts into which the bolts are screwed, through the chassis rail. A helping hand is useful at this point. Slide the towbar into the chassis rails and secure the forward-most bolts first. This supports the bar and makes it easier to align the front bolts. Insert all of the bolts and check that the bar is level before tightening. There is no recommended torque – suffice it to say that you want them tight.

Wiring tails connect directly to the factory wiring harness.

The bumper iron itself is held on by two 13mm bolts each side. Remove these and lift it out of the way. With the bumper removed you can see inside the chassis legs. Note that there are three bolt holes on the inner wall – this is where the towbar will attach.

The towbar is secured using three large bolts.

Remove the large tail-light wiring grommet.

useful extras

Once the bar is in place it is time for the electrics. The kit came with a right- and a left-side loom, which simply clip into the existing lighting plugs, as well as comprehensive instructions. Push the existing wiring grommet into the body; this allows access to feed the wiring down to the bumper area.

Lower grommet for the towbar plug wiring.

Feed a stiff piece of wire down the inside of the panel.

Pull through the wiring and fit the supplied grommet.

At the bottom corner of the body you will find a small rubber grommet. Remove this and then take a stiff piece of wire and feed it up through the lower hole until you can see it appear at the upper hole. This can be a very frustrating task, so be patient. Tape the wiring loom to the stiff wire and pull it down and out of the lower hole. The kit included rubber grommets to replace the existing solid ones. With the wire fed through, route it to the centre of the towbar and secure it with cable ties.

The wiring needed a dedicated earth point fitting.

The loom also features an earth wire that is supposed to attach to an earth point behind the rear-most interior panel. However, we could not access this without ripping out the carpet lining. Instead, we added an earth connection using a threaded insert behind the lighting panel.

Do not forget to feed the plug wiring through the plug bracket.

useful extras

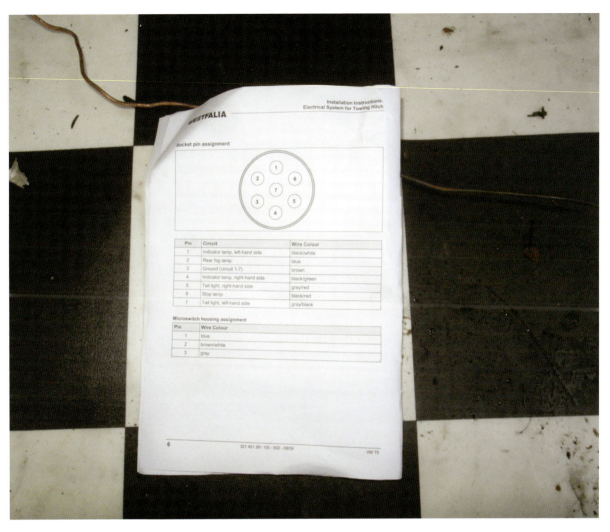

A wiring diagram was supplied with the kit.

Once you have completed this process on both sides of the vehicle it is time to connect the plug. Do not forget to feed the wires through the plug mounting plate and backing grommet before attaching them to the plug. The kit came with a clear wiring diagram for the plug. Each terminal is numbered and it is simply a matter of matching the wire colour to the correct number. The plug also features a microswitch to disable parking sensors, if they are fitted.

Attach the cables to their respective connectors.

The final result: a towbar that should prove very useful.

Check that all the lights function as they should.

At the end, if you have wires left over, go back and check the instructions as they should all have a home. With everything connected, secure the plug plate and then you will have a nicely fitted towbar. The final job is to check that everything works properly. You should have a trailer indicator on the dashboard that activates when additional load is put on the wiring system. If your trailer has any lights out, this will not operate, so make sure they all work.

index

adhesive 43
amps 99
appliances
   kitchen units 64
   selection 88

battery 105
beds
   fitting 72
   options 71
   rock and roll 71
   roof bed 82
   upholstery 75
bodywork
   T4 10
   T5 13
brake fluid 13
budget 19
buying 8

cables
   conduit 104
   construction 99
   joints 100
   selection 99
   specifications 99
California 7
carpet lining 44
chassis
   T4 9
   T5 12
chassis plate 13
circular saw 21
cooker 90
coolant 14
crimps 100
cupboards 66
current flow 97

drawers 66

electrics 97
electric circuits 97
electric formula 98
engines
   T4 8
   T5 11

flooring 48
foam 75
fridges
furniture board 52

gas
   canister 91
   fridge 89
   introduction 88
   installation 91
   regulator 91
   safety 89, 93
   types 90
gearbox
   T4 9
   T5 11
ground 98

hole saw 21

insulation
   floor 50
   walls 42
insurance 23
interior lights 113
interior sockets 110
interior units
   construction 55
   plans 53, 54, 56

jigsaw 21

knock-on edging 61

latches 69

mains power 107
mains safety 108
materials
   general 22
   sound proofing 42
   units 52
MDF 52
multimeter 100

ohms 99
optional extras 13

planning 18
plywood
   hardwood 52
   lightweight 53
power management system 106
power steering 14

reclassification 23
reversing camera 118
roof
   fitting 25
   types 25
router 21

safety 24
service history 8
sink fitting 65
soldering 101
splicing 102
stereo installation 116
swivel seat 79

T25 8
tambour doors 60
time 22
tools 20
towbar 120

upholstery 75

vinyl 76
volt 99
voltage drop 100

wardrobe 57
water supply 93
watts 99
windows
   cutting 36
   selection 35
worktop 64
   fitting 39

RELATED TITLES FROM CROWOOD

Fitting a Camper Van Interior
ROB HAWKINS
ISBN 978 1 84797 605 5
160pp, 750 illustrations

Volkswagen T4 1990–2003
RICHARD COPPING
ISBN 978 1 84797 554 6
208pp, 300 illustrations

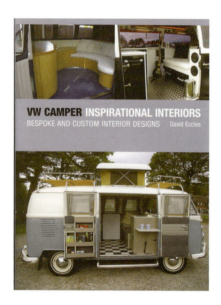

VW Camper – Inspirational Interiors
DAVID ECCLES
ISBN 978 1 84797 070 1
224pp, 400 illustrations

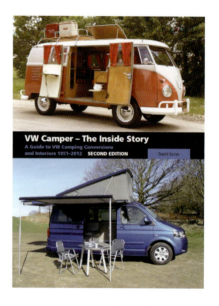

VW Camper – The Inside Story
DAVID ECCLES
ISBN 978 1 84797 417 4
192pp, 500 illustrations

In case of difficulty ordering, please contact the Sales Office:

The Crowood Press
Ramsbury
Wiltshire
SN8 2HR
UK

Tel: 44 (0) 1672 520320

enquiries@crowood.com

www.crowood.com